MW00996422

COWBOY
BARBECUE

COWBOY
BARBECUE

FIRE & SMOKE FROM THE
ORIGINAL TEXAS VAQUEROS

ADRIAN DAVILA
with ANN VOLKWEIN

The Countryman Press

A division of W. W. Norton & Company

Independent Publishers Since 1923

Copyright © 2018 by Adrian Davila
Photographs © 2018 by Pauline Stevens

All rights reserved
Printed in the United States of America

For information about permission to reproduce selections from this book, write to
Permissions, The Countryman Press, 500 Fifth Avenue, New York, NY 10110

For information about special discounts for bulk purchases, please contact
W. W. Norton Special Sales at specialsales@wwnorton.com or 800-233-4830

Manufacturing by Versa Press
Book design by LeAnna Weller Smith
Production manager: Devon Zahn

The Countryman Press
www.countrymanpress.com

A division of W. W. Norton & Company, Inc.
500 Fifth Avenue, New York, NY 10110
www.wwnorton.com

978-1-68268-142-8 (pbk.)

10 9 8 7 6 5 4 3 2 1

To all the people who have made food like this over the centuries, and to the vaqueros whose voices were never heard, I am honored to have this chance to celebrate them through our recipes and stories.

CONTENTS

Smoked Pulled Pork 73

Pork Loin with Mustard Seed Sauce 74

Puerco en Chili Colorado (*Pork in Red Chili Sauce*) 76

Smoked Ham with Davila's BBQ Sauce Glaze 79

Morcilla (*Spanish Blood Sausage*) 81

Chicharonnes en Salsa Verde 83

Mole de Olla con Puerco 84

POULTRY

Whole Mesquite-Smoked Chicken 85

Chicken Fajitas 87

Tinga de Pollo 89

Calabacita con Pollo (*Squash with Chicken*) 91

Arroz con Pollo (*Rice with Chicken*) 92

Brined and Smoked Whole Turkey 94

South Texas Peanut Butter Mole 95

Seafood 97

Camarones al Mojo de Ajo (*Shirmp in Garlic Sauce*) 98

Mexican Shrimp and Oyster Cocktail 100

Aguachiles de Camarones (*Shrimp in Chili Broth*) 101

Smoked Fresh Oysters 102

Texas Gulf Ceviche-Stuffed Avocados 103

Caribbean-Style Whole Red Snapper 104

Glazed Barbecued Salmon 106

Street Foods 109

MINI TACOS

Tacos al Pastor *(Pineapple and Pork)* 110

Tacos de Birria (*Goat*) 112

Tacos Campechanos (*Beef with Chorizo and Chicharrones*) 114

Tacos de Buche *(Pork Stomach)* 116

Tripas de Res Tacos (*Beef Tripe*) 117

TAMALES

Tamales Verdes *(Chicken with Green Sauce)* 120

Tamales Rojos (*Pork with Red Sauce*) 122

Tamales Rajas de Chile y Queso Fresco (*Chile and Cheese*) 124

Soups and Chilis 127

Mama Davila's Fideo Seco con Carne 128

Caldo de Res 129

Sopa de Fideo Estilo Laredo 130

Chicken Tortilla Soup 132

Pozole Rojo de Puerco (*Red Pork Pozole*) 133

Vaquero Chili con Carne 134

Menudo de Puerco 136

Pozole Verde de Pollo (*Green Chicken Pozole*) 138

ON THE SIDE

INTRODUCTION

THE DAVILA FAMILY HISTORY, FROM ÁVILA TO SEGUIN

Long before the first smoker was lit or sauce was ladled, barbecue was born with a Latin twist. The oft-forgotten vaquero origins of this meat-heavy and nomad-friendly style of cooking are the focus of this book, celebrating the greatest culinary traditions of Latin America, and rediscovering my family's heritage along the way.

As a third-generation member of the Davila's BBQ family, my style of cooking evolved from a strong base of family recipes and the rich culture that surrounds me in South Texas. But as I have explored my roots more deeply, I've discovered my culinary references reach back to the vaqueros, the horsemen on the Iberian Peninsula who shepherded the prized cattle to the wide open lands of the New World.

At Davila's BBQ, we've always known how good our cooking is, as we've been serving the Seguin, Texas, community for three generations now. But in recent years I've had the opportunity to travel, do some television and print media, and help give my hometown, Seguin, its rightful place on the BBQ map. To bring our historically important, Latin-influenced barbecue to a wider audience is supremely gratifying. *Cowboy Barbecue* feels like a natural progression in my journey as a chef, to write about my food and share my recipes while exploring the Old World techniques that I've mastered. What I didn't anticipate at the start of writing this book was just how far the journey and my research into my family history were going to take me.

It All Began with This Man: My Grandfather, the Original Pit Master

My great-grandfather had a general store in the renowned barbecue town of Luling, Texas, in the 1930s and 1940s. My grandfather, Raul Davila, and his brother Adolph worked at the store but didn't want people assuming they had not earned their own way, so at the age of 14 and 12 respectively, Raul and Adolph got on a train headed west into the Hill Country, to work in a restaurant in Kerrville, Texas. When they reached their 20s, they returned to town to work at the Bob Davis Locker Processing Plant, as butchers and sausage makers. This was where they started to hone their culinary skills, learning Polish (adds garlic and spices) and German (simply seasoned and smoked) sausage-making techniques from the source as well as smoking techniques for barbecue. These European immigrants came to colonize Texas beginning in the 1830s, bringing with them their food traditions (and blending Polish polka and accordions into the South Texas music!).

By the 1950s, my uncle and grandfather were selling their sausages and barbecue out of my uncle's very own dry goods and convenience store to joints from Lockhart to San Antonio. It wasn't long before Raul and my grandmother, Geronima, opened up their own place in Luling, named the Carnation Restaurant, serving barbecue and Mexican food. Raul added cayenne and other ingredients to give the sausage and barbecue his own Latin twist. At the time Seguin was the county seat and a more populated city than Luling, so my grandfather's next move was to strike a deal to open a new barbecue place in an old abandoned schoolhouse in Seguin in September 1959. No decorations, no cash register, and the whole family slept in two of the rooms at the back of restaurant. (To this day my father doesn't ever want to leave the restaurant, because it's home to him, even

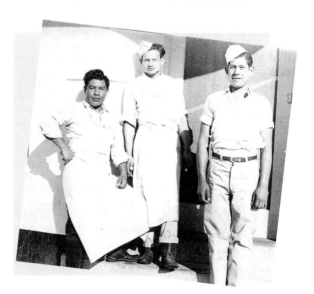

Left to right: Mike Hernandez, Adolph Davila (my great-uncle), and Guadalupe Gonzalez, circa 1948 at the Bob Davis Locker Plant.

in its newer location.) Raul built a pit outside and added a few tables inside. They were happy to be the first restaurant, outside of African American–owned establishments, to serve African Americans in a public space in Seguin. In the 1970s, sausage making became so busy that they moved that part of the operation to its own building.

But there's no doubt that the restaurant exists today due to my grandmother's jumping in whenever needed. She grew up on a working cattle ranch, which her father tended. They had their own pigs and grew all their own vegetables. She had only an elementary school education, but she figured out how to run the restaurant. And she made enchiladas and tamales as well as the barbecue on the menu. Her hard work was all about putting food on the table; after all, she had three kids to feed. Even today, she is still the taskmaster and the backbone of the family.

My Story: Third-Generation Pit Master

I always wanted to be around my dad, Edward Davila, and my dad was always at the restaurant, working as my grandfather's right-hand man and starting the concession and catering side of the business. The meat would come in and I'd watch my grandfather break down a quarter of a cow, do the butchering

MY COUSIN: TEX DAVILA MCLEOD

One of the more colorful characters in my family history is my cousin Tex McLeod. I've often thought that his legacy is responsible for sending me on this vaquero-inspired journey in the first place. Tex was a cowboy who took his spin ropes all the way from South Texas to the Calgary Stampede, a world championship cowboy competition in Alberta, Canada, at which he won the "All-Around Cowboy" title in the 1920s. After traveling with Buffalo Bill's Wild West show, he moved to England and had a second career as a famous silent film star in the 1930s. He went on to travel the world, teaching "ropes and yarns" to African kings and English royalty. His legacy as a showman and an explorer inspired me to want to follow in his footsteps, using my craft in cooking as my means of exploration, to do and see things that I had never done or seen before, as he did with his skills as a cowboy. Growing up, I was secluded in South Texas, but his story encouraged me to scour maps and use a globe, filled with the certainty that these challenges and adventures were mine to have. I've found that the rugged essence of the western way of life that captivated Tex McLeod's contemporaries is no less fascinating to the outside world today.

and sausage making, and then take it all into the smoker. I'd also sit out in the front of the restaurant, to watch people smile and enjoy the food. I loved the process of creating memories. Gathering over food with friends and family, you always remember what you eat and who you eat it with. I fell in love with creating that experience for people. I would hide in the catering van at four in the morning and wait quietly until my dad arrived at the catering spot, to try to skip school and be with him. At six or seven years old, I'd stir the huge vats of scrambled eggs. I liked being part of the process.

Throughout my high school years, I was very involved in sports and not in the restaurant as much. But when I went to college, I realized the classroom setting wasn't ever going to work with my ADD, and my dad suggested I get to work. I began full-time at the restaurant but, like my grandfather, I didn't want the stigma of having something given to me, so I started working in the pits. Then, I opened a series of satellite locations over the course of the next 15 years, and even had a food truck for a while, which helped me to experiment with types of food I could cater. The key has been to keep evolving and growing, while still coming back and tending to the core business when needed. (And recently, I brought the food truck back!)

The Davila Inquisition

There are always a few generations of voices in my head, which serve as a constant reminder to work hard. It's a matter of family pride. I've felt a strong desire to learn more about my heritage, and I've always had a nagging feeling that there was more to discover. In 2016, I visited Ávila, Spain, seeking my roots. What moved me the most was uncovering a profound connection between my passion for our style of cooking and the flavors of the Iberian Peninsula. The spit style of cooking; decidedly un-Texan ingredients, such as lamb (which nonetheless we serve at Davila's); and the way they seasoned their mashed potatoes with tomato sauce and a crunch of *chicharrones* mixed in, felt familiar. We happened to visit one of the main historical attractions in the city, the Palacio de los Dávila, built by (I found out later) a distant aristocratic ancestor, Pedrarias Dávila. He led the first great Spanish expedition in the New World, further sparking my interest in the ties between my world and the Old World.

Back in Seguin with my friend and mentor, Julia Rosenfeld, who teaches a food history class at the Culinary Institute of America in San Antonio, I began thinking more deeply about why my family, seemingly so well situated in Spain, had left in the first place. After hearing about how my family emigrated in the 1600s, came to Peru as merchants, then kept on moving, heading northward, through the centuries, Julia wondered whether the Davila family had branched and that my ancestors were in fact Jewish. After all, they'd left during the Spanish Inquisition and Ávila was known throughout the Crusades as a place where all three ideologies, Muslim, Catholic, and Jewish, were represented, and in conflict. Intrigued, I found a cousin who had been studying our family history for the last decade. He confirmed that the Iberian Davilas were in fact Jewish, to his knowledge, and that they were horse traders, likely dealing with the vaqueros who were brought originally from Spain and trained in the Iberian tradition to become North America's original cowboys, and with the Catholic missions that owned and drove the cattle business.

My mind was blown. As far back as anyone could remember, my family and community had always been very involved in the Catholic Church, and I had never heard of the Jewish connection. We were not aware of a Jewish community or synagogue in our town—and my family has property tax records in Seguin going back to 1872. But examining the oldest photo I own of a Davila, of my great-great-grandfather, in 1892, with his big beard and round hat, it wasn't all that hard to imagine. Mestizos, those of mixed European and Native American descent, didn't have facial hair, and to me he looks like someone from the Basque country—but he was in Texas. I felt in my bones that this history explained some of my attraction to the vaqueros and their way of life, and my curiosity about the cultural influences grew even stronger. In some ways it made perfect sense; the Spanish brought horses to the New World, after all. The power of the Catholic Church in the region, and a history of persecution, could easily explain why my family eventually buried their original Jewish heritage. For example, the Catholic missionaries methodically tried to suppress native Indian customs, including an attempt at breaking down their societal structure through food. In the mid-1800s, they banned the cultivation of corn and encouraged the planting of wheat for flour. It wasn't just about changing their diet; the Indian culture was connected to the corn harvest and the flow of the seasons, as a form of worship. Needless to say, it wasn't a very successful law, and many revolted immediately, but even when the ban was lifted, there was still a stigma attached to it—and I grew up eating mostly flour tortillas, as did my grandmother.

I have more research to do on our origins, but to be able to draw a line from my ancestors' work, to my grandfather

My outdoor kitchen at the ranch, looking west towards Seguin.

as a butcher, our barbecue restaurant, all the way to me today, living on a working cattle ranch and marrying a rancher's daughter, was astounding to me. There I had it, right underneath my feet, on my own trail. The strong entrepreneurship in my family, the risk-taking—I know where it all comes from now. We will live and die among the longhorns. The photographs for this book were shot at our restaurant and on our land. Many recognize the profoundly delicious and famous products of Hill Country barbecue, but in *Cowboy Barbecue*, I celebrate South Texas, and all the layers of Latin influence, techniques, and ingredients are finally given their due. Can you smell the mesquite?

THE VAQUERO WAY

Tracing my family history from Ávila, Spain, to present-day Peru, traveling north toward what is now northern Mexico, I imagine how they used the native ingredients available, adapting them to their cooking techniques and bringing them to their tables. When they weren't roasting meat while on the move, these Spanish immigrants drew together a cuisine from an often-unforgiving land: of *nopales* (cactus paddles), *tripas* (tripe), blood sausage . . .

Vaqueros were really shepherds, herding their cattle from grassland to fresh grassland, constantly on the move. With no home base, these men of the land were married to the cows. Ingredients had to be portable. It wasn't until 1809 that food started to be canned (by a Frenchman named Appert), so such things as beans, flour or masa, and rice were staples to buy when they'd come into town to stock up on provisions before their long rides. To this day, the simple staples of tortillas, beans, and rice form the center of our tables all over our region. The vaqueros cooked over an open fire, using the mesquite wood they'd gather. A designated forager and trapper would bring them the occasional turkey, quail, rabbit, dove, or snake, and they might occasionally be allotted a calf by the cattle owners. But eating beef, pork, or chicken was most often reserved for celebratory *asados* (open-fire barbecues) and special occasions.

The original vaqueros had a deeply independent spirit and profound connection to the cattle and the land itself that is still found in the vaqueros of today. These herdsmen on horseback inspire my passion as I explore the Mexican-, Spanish-, and American-influenced barbecue traditions that are widely enjoyed in South Texas and celebrated since 1959 at Davila's BBQ.

My Way—
The Vaquero Mash-Up

The vaquero way of cooking entails using what is plentiful and readily available, while being resourceful and incorporating every part of the plant or animal. This ultimate respect for the land and its inhabitants translates into cooking with great passion and great results. Eating organs and tougher cuts of meat led to "low and slow" cooking, rubs, wraps, and other methods necessary to soften the meat or infuse it with spices to enhance its flavor. It's within these methods that it's possible to trace the influences in the food the vaqueros made. These techniques and flavorings crossed many lands and oceans to form the vaquero-style food that we know today.

Mollejas (sweetbreads, page 44), Tripas de Res (tripe, page 117), Fire-Roasted Tomato, Onion, and Serrano Salsa (page 174), camotes (sweet potatoes) cooked directly on coals (page 155), the oregano and cumin added to our spicy BBQ sauce (page 173), and the cayenne added to our rub (page 43) . . . these elements help form the essence of our

Opposite top: Grilling up fajitas and peppers, and cooking butternut squash and foil-wrapped sweet potatoes in the coals.

Opposite bottom: Family and friends enjoying a moment before the meal.

food at Davila's. One of our most popular dishes is a recipe that you won't find on any typical barbecue menu in Texas: Mesquite-Smoked Lamb Ribs (page 65). I take the lamb breast, a relatively low-cost cut of meat, and envelop it in the mesquite-scented heat of our pit, slow-cooking it and basting in its juices to produce the most tender rib with just the right amount of flavorful, rubbed crust. I like to serve it with my version of chimichurri sauce, with roasted bell peppers and serrano pepper, because the tang and bite of the sauce cuts through the fatty, smoky, savory ribs.

Beyond the tried-and-true staples that we serve at the restaurant, I have explored a wide range of cooking techniques through my catering business and at my home. For example, upon coming to the New World, the Spanish were taught by locals to cook meat wrapped in maguey leaves in a pit in the ground; it's then steamed slowly by the heat of the wood coals to create a rustic, original style of *barbacoa* (page 54). I was inspired to dig a permanent underground pit in my backyard for barbacoa and learned to cook whole fish in banana leaves and to harness the gaucho-style spitfires and asado style of cooking meat and vegetables directly on the embers for authentic and outstanding flavor.

Whole-Animal Cooking and Slow Food

Through travel and friends I seek out the authentic, old ways of doing things. Recently, I was invited to central Mexico to attend the funeral of a friend and longtime employee. I arrived in Tlanchinol in the dead of night, having traveled for 6 hours up into the mountains outside of Mexico City. As I entered the main house, there were some 50 to 75 people praying the rosary over the body, a ritual that would continue until morning. At about 4 a.m., I retired to sleep in the upper house. Two hours later, I awoke to the cry of a rooster, and saw that there must have been two dozen people sleeping in beds and on the floor around me. Suddenly, I heard screeches like I've never heard before. A bit disoriented, I made my way across the room and opened the door of the house. Mind you I had arrived in the dark, so was struck by the view that stretched thousands of feet down the mountains spread out before me, dotted with mountain villages. To my right, four men were wrangling a 200-pound pig.

Opposite top left: Checking the barbacoa fresh out of the in-ground pit.

Opposite top right: Cutting up fajitas while Goose (left) and Oso (right) hope for a treat to drop.

Opposite bottom: Jalapeño corn bread cooking over the fire outdoors.

Traditions run deep up in the mountains, and cooking a whole pig for a funeral is a communal process. The livestock is a valuable gift given to pay homage to the deceased, usually presented to the family by a neighbor. I witnessed the ritual of slaughtering the pig. The gentleman in charge of breaking down the carcass showed me bit by bit how to do it, by hand, with a respect and pride that was almost religious in nature. Nothing was wasted, not even a single drop of blood, which was used in sausage along with the innards. The women used the meat from the head, cheek, and jowls to make tamales, the skin was used to make chicharrones, the stomach was stuffed with rice and organ meat, the main body was barbecued, and the legs were cooked underground. Food was central to the gathering, with everyone participating in the preparations, and even young kids had the important job of bringing the wood to keep the fire going for hours. There was a sense of accomplishment in the air over the course of the day, of working together to honor the deceased and the mourning family members, sharing stories and creating new memories. Everyone played their part, down to the *banda* players, with their tuba, trumpets, and horns, who led the funeral procession. The feast ultimately served 80 to 100 people. In Latin culture, our stomach always soothes us.

I didn't know where this book would take me when I started, but I knew I was looking for answers about our food and where I came from. I learned far more than I expected, and it changed me. One of the most enduring lessons is just how much the modern food industry has changed our everyday lives. We hardly see the process, much less the cultivation and the harvesting involved in what we eat today. My friends and crew from the restaurant shared so much with me, teaching ancient methods of cooking, from harvesting maguey to in-ground barbacoa, and joined me for endless hours, prepping masa for tamales and turning the pig roast. It has reconnected me to the food of our heritage and brought me into the social circle that is intrinsic to this type of slow food, made by communities.

What I value most about this experience is tapping into our DNA, our makeup, as Latinos and as South Texans, honoring ancient techniques and native ingredients from the vaqueros of my heritage. It's not the way everyone does it, but it is who I am. It's my soul food. Welcome to *Cowboy Barbecue*.

Opposite top left: Sarah serving fresh jalapeño cornbread, cooked in a cast-iron skillet over the coals.

Opposite top right: The pure joy of cooking outdoors.

Opposite bottom: Working the coals to make them hotter to ensure the pig skin crisps up for chicharrones.

TECHNIQUES ON FIRE

To go direct or indirect, that is the basic question. I assume at the beginning everything was just put on the fire to cook, until the day someone figured out that if you move the meat a little away from the flames, it's possible to grill with more finesse, and if you move it even farther away, then the smoke from the fire will eventually break down muscle tissues. Smoking a big piece of meat for 9 to 10 hours can turn a very tough cut into something spectacularly moist and tender. On the opposite end of the spectrum, by grilling lean cuts over high direct heat, asado style, you can obtain just the right flavor from the fire—as long as you don't overcook it. Well, we get to benefit from the trials and tribulations of others and are blessed with the knowledge of what to use when and how to build the perfect indirect and direct fires. It's my privilege to share this with you.

DIRECT HEAT: ASADO STYLE

As much as meat is the center of the table today in South Texas, the rough vaquero lifestyle was a humble existence where meat was not an everyday part of the meal. For the most part, their time was spent tending the cattle, not grilling it, and they had to keep moving on to greener pastures to feed the herd. The constant movement also prevented them from having domesticated pigs and chickens. So, when they had the occasion to grill, they made it special. To this day, an asado, in Latin culture, is a social event.

Preferably, for asado-style cooking, you use a charcoal grill with hardwood charcoal and a cast-iron grate, as outlined in the following technique. An open propane or gas grill can deliver direct heat just as well, but you won't have the same flavor profile.

TOOLS

· Chimney starter
· Fuel (wood or charcoal) of your choice (see notes)
· Quick-reading, meat probe thermometer
· Long tongs
· Long grilling spatula
· Water bottle, cap on, with a hole poked in the top (for flare-ups or to cool "too hot" coals so that the meat doesn't char)
· Refillable butane lighter

Depending on your recipe and the level of heat and the amount of coals needed, you have to burn wood for varying amounts of time before it's ready to cook your asado. For example, some recipes, such as tacos al pastor or fajitas, you will need to burn the wood/charcoal for 30 to 45 minutes for it to become white hot, other recipes, such as the whole-head barbacoa, you will need to burn the wood/charcoal for 2 to 3 hours before your fire is ready.

1. Put the starter on a safe, heatproof surface. The best location is on the grate of the grill prior to heating it up. That way, if anything falls in, it's going to the right place—where you will dump it out later.

2. Stuff a few pieces of bunched-up newspaper in the bottom side of the chimney and fill the top almost all the way with the wood of your choice or natural charcoal.

3. Light the newspaper in the bottom of the chimney and let it burn; the flames from the newspaper will light the wood/charcoal in the top.

4. When the wood/charcoal is lit and flames are barely licking out of the top, dump the wood/charcoal right in the middle of your grill or barbecue pit and follow the recipe as to what level of heat your coals need to be before cooking.

NOTES: If using wood, use completely dry (cured) wood—it can be cherry wood, mesquite, hickory, or pecan. The vaqueros used whatever wood they found around them, and at my restaurant in Seguin, we use mesquite wood because it is readily available in the area.

If you need to do two-zone grilling and don't have an indirect smoker, see the following method.

INDIRECT HEAT: SMOKING

Indirect heat allows for a longer cooking process, by providing just enough heat for the fat to render to the surface of the meat and breaking down the connective tissue with smoke and heat to make it tender. The temperature has to be just right: If you cook it too high, you will bake the meat and it will become tough and dry, and if you cook it too low, the meat will dry out slowly, because the fat won't render properly. You know you're doing your job right when the meat is glistening with fat. Get it right, or your ribs will turn out orange instead of the correct deep maroon, your chicken will be white instead of golden caramel, and your brisket will appear hard and yellow instead of dark with a smoke ring.

TOOLS

· Fuel (wood) of your choice (see previous notes for direct heat)
· Quick-reading, meat probe thermometer
· Long tongs
· Long grilling spatula
· Refillable butane lighter

When to start the fire for indirect smoking depends on the pit or grill that you're working with. Heating up a big pit or grill when it's cold outside will take longer than a small pit on a hot day. Generally it can take about 30 minutes after lighting to burn down the wood and heat it up, then you put a second layer of thicker wood to create the smoke for the meat. Meanwhile, get your meat close to room temperature.

A barbecue pit with natural logs is ideal for smoking. An alternative is to buy a smoker that uses pellets. You can also buy gadgets that plug in and blow smoke. But the easiest way to smoke meat without a pit is to set up a grill with two zones, with the fire on the side, as described here. You get radiant heat and lots of good smoke.

1. Refer to the sidebar "Placement of the Wood," page 31, for the shape of your grill. Stack the wood in a tower form by starting with your largest two logs, placing them at the bottom, parallel to each other with some space in between, to create a base. Ideally, you want the size of the logs to decrease as you make your tower. Put the next largest two logs horizontally across the first two logs, parallel to each other with some space in between. Continue this until you have made a tower of logs that is two-thirds of the way up the side below the grill grate.

PLACEMENT *of the* WOOD

The most important part of the indirect-heat, fire-building process is the placement of the wood in a designated spot in your grill.

For a rectangular grill: Stack the wood on one side of the grill, so that about half of the grill will be filled with wood.

For a square grill: Stack one-third of your grill with wood.

For a circular grill: Line one half of the grill with a crescent shape of stacked logs, touching the side. A circular grill is not ideal for indirect smoking, but if you pay close attention to the placement of the logs and the heat, then you will be fine.

HOW *to* GAUGE *the* GRILL TEMPERATURE

High: When you place your hand 8 inches above the grill grates and you immediately have to take it away because of the heat (about 500°F).

Medium: When you place your hand 8 inches about the grill grates and you can tolerate 1 to 2 seconds of heat without pulling your hand back (about 350°F).

Low: When you place your hand 8 inches above the grill and can tolerate 3 to 4 seconds of heat without pulling your hand back (about 250°F).

HOW *to* CLEAN *a* GRILL

The best way to remove the leftover grit and food particles on your grill is to use an onion! My simple, all-natural method: Cut a large onion in half, crosswise. Grab half of it and rub down length of grill, following the lines of the grates. It's just like cleaning a plate in your sink.

2. The best way to get your fire started is to use lit coals from a chimney starter to light the wood you will be using. Light your chimney starter as you would for an asado fire (see page 28). Then simply dump the lit coals from the chimney starter in the middle of the tower of logs. Most will fall to the bottom and the coals will light the logs. Allow the logs to burn down, a maximum of 30 to 45 minutes, until they form coals, and you're ready to cook.

SMOKING MEAT THE DAVILA WAY

Today a lot of pit masters use barrel-style, cast-iron smoking pits. The wood burns in a partially closed firebox on one end, the meat is on a grate in the middle, and the flue is on the opposite end. The flue exhausts the smoke, controlling the temperature and the smoke amount. With the flue on the opposite end from the fire's heat, these pits draw the billowing smoke across the meat. Most retail barbecue pits are scaled down versions of the barrel-style pits.

My grandfather built our pits with his hands, out of cinderblock and steel. We use hot coals and walk the line between smoking and open-fire direct cooking. In our pits, the heat and smoke from the hot mesquite is directed around the meat. This is how we do it: our pit is more like an industrial smoker; a firebrick-lined, concrete-filled mason block structure with two sets of cast-iron metal doors to access the meat stacked on two big lazy Susans, flanking the fire. There is a third set of cast-iron doors in the middle where the firebox is, and two side flues. But the pit is all one big room, so the fire is in the same space as the meat. It's more like the two-zone indirect cooking I describe earlier, where the meat is next to the fire, and almost

Left: Brisket cooking on the original old smoker.

Opposite top: Grandpa Raul and my father, Edward, standing proud in front of a cart full of brisket, circa 1984.

Opposite bottom: In front of our lazy Susan–style pits, designed and made by hand by Grandpa Raul

flame kissed, instead of partially closed off. The result is a searing effect, almost like asado or campfire cooking, with just a perfume of mesquite. There's a convection oven quality, not the huge clouds of smoke that you find in barrel-style cookers. This setup creates a lot of radiant heat. Cook times are therefore a little bit faster than in a traditional smoker, with chicken and ribs taking 3 hours, and brisket, 10, as opposed to 16 to 18 hours. In some barbecue all you taste is smoke. That's not our style; we want you to taste the meat and the seasonings.

The best way to approximate our method is to use the indirect-heat method, using two zones (see page 30).

Above: Dad loading up the van for one of our first catering jobs, a wedding, in 1972.

Opposite top left: Me and Alex Perez preparing to lower our lamb in the pozo (hole)–style pit.

Opposite top right: Sarah, ready to make salsa verde.

Opposite bottom: My extended family, with my grandmother Davila, the matriarch, front and center.

MAINS

MEAT ON FIRE

In South Texas, meat is always the star of the dish. My entire life I have been surrounded by meats of all kinds, from the restaurant stock to catering orders, which included venison, lamb, and whole beef heads.

    Walking into our meat cooler as a young boy, at any given time I was bound to come in contact with a whole animal among the hanging, aging, or cut meats. In many ways, meat was the center of my life. I'd help my grandfather break down and butcher whole animals and became familiar with all the cuts of beef and pork. And I got excited finding new ways to cook a whole animal or its parts, as well as making popular dishes. As a result . . . this chapter runs the gauntlet from a brined center-cut pork loin to the national dish of Texas, brisket.

MESQUITE BRISKET

SERVES 15 TO 20   PREP TIME: 12 TO 24 HOURS   COOK TIME: 11 TO 12 HOURS

A staple dish of Texas, brisket can take on so many personalities. It is great on the plate, in an enchilada, or on a sandwich, baked potatoes, or Frito pie. Everything goes with brisket in Texas. Nothing goes to waste, as even the burnt ends are prized. Take it from me; I have battered and deep-fried a brisket (no joke) just to change it up a bit. A well-smoked section taken from the lean end is just as juicy and flavorful as any steak. The fatty, marbled meat soaks up the seasonings and tastes like something between roast beef and barbacoa. Everything is bigger and in Texas and nothing is bigger in the BBQ world than brisket.

With so many different smokers, techniques, and approaches, this traditional recipe is often overcomplicated in our world today. Our recipe requires no basting, wrapping, no special magic or trickery, but it has stood the test of time in one of the most competitive BBQ markets in the country. For more than 60 years and three generations, my family has prepared brisket this way. We keep it simple and we love it. And . . . people keep coming back for more.

If you don't have a pit: You can slow cook the meat in the oven at 275°F for 8 hours.

1 beef brisket (12 to 14 pounds), untrimmed

1¼ cups Davila's Signature BBQ Rub (recipe follows)

1. Put the brisket in a large plastic tub and generously apply Davila's BBQ Rub all over the brisket, ensuring that all crevices and uneven surfaces are covered.

2. Cover the tub and refrigerate for 12 to 24 hours; 24 hours is ideal for the full absorption of the seasoning due to the thickness of the meat.

3. Thirty to 45 minutes before you want to cook, prepare the pit or grill for an indirect smoking method of cooking (see page 30).

continued

Knowing how to cut the brisket is equally as important as knowing how to cook it, because a perfectly cooked brisket can be ruined if cut improperly. Cutting against the grain ensures smooth slices that are juicy, tender, and flavorful. Don't let your long, hard work go to waste.

For optimal flavor and results, use large logs on the fire and maintain the fire's temperature, so that you have an equal amount of smoke and heat.

4. Put the brisket on the rack in the pit with the fat side up and the larger end facing the fire source. (The larger end needs to face the fire as it is thicker and takes longer to cook. If you place the smaller end of the brisket closer to the fire, it will cook faster and the brisket will cook unevenly.)

5. Turn the brisket (flip it) every 2 hours. Make sure to use gloves to turn. Do not use a fork because each time you puncture the brisket, you will lose some of the juice and it may become too dry. Cook the meat until it is completely tender (and jiggles when you shake it), 11 to 12 hours total.

6. Remove the brisket from the heat and allow it to rest for 35 to 45 minutes before slicing against the grain. Serve.

NOTE: The smaller the brisket, the leaner it is; you want your brisket big and fat. Regardless of whether you eat the fat, you can trim it away, but it's essential for the meat to cook in its juices. The brisket is made up of two muscles. The top cap is what you call the "moist" and the bottom is the "lean" flat part. You can buy smaller briskets, but you have to buy one that still has fat on it. You can use a 6-pound brisket; just reduce the cook time by 30 to 40 percent.

DAVILA'S SIGNATURE BBQ RUB

MAKES **2 CUPS**

1½ cups salt

⅓ cup freshly ground black
  pepper

3 tablespoons cayenne pepper

In Texas, most BBQ purists let the meat speak for itself by only seasoning with salt and pepper. We add cayenne for a natural Latin kick. In the restaurant, we use this to enhance the robustness of lamb or beef, complement inherently sweet pork, or lend a flavor boost to milder chicken recipes.

1. Thoroughly mix the salt, black pepper, and cayenne together in a bowl.
2. Rub on any meat to add a kick of flavor. Store in an airtight container.

MOLLEJAS (SWEETBREADS)

MAKES **6 TO 8 TACOS**   PREP TIME: **5 TO 10 MINUTES PREP, PLUS 3 TO 4 HOURS TO MARINATE**

COOK TIME: **30 TO 40 MINUTES**

When properly trimmed and prepped, soaked, and boiled, sweetbreads lose the gamey flavor that turn off some people and you're left with a clean, meaty taste. They're often overlooked and undervalued in today's culinary world, but this cut is truly a delicacy, prized by chefs for centuries. There are only two glands per animal. It's a bit costly to prepare, yet the reward is rich and you'll be another step closer to ensuring nothing gets wasted, for every part of the animal has been made useful.

1 pound mollejas (sweetbreads, preferably the "belly" section of the thymus gland)

½ cup white vinegar

Salt

½ cup plain yogurt

4 garlic cloves, chopped

2 serrano peppers, sliced

Freshly ground black pepper

2 lemons, halved

Eight 6- to 8-inch flour tortillas

Sliced avocado and Pico de Gallo (page 183) for serving

Grilled onion and tomatoes (optional)

1. Put the mollejas, vinegar, and 1 teaspoon of salt in a medium saucepan over high heat, and add water to cover. Bring to a boil and cook until they become white and puffy, 8 to 10 minutes.

2. Drain the water from the saucepan and cover the meat with ice to stop the cooking process.

3. Mix together the yogurt, garlic, serrano peppers, 1 teaspoon of salt, and 1 teaspoon of black pepper in a large, resealable plastic bag or sealable plastic container. Add the mollejas and allow to marinate in the refrigerator for 3 to 4 hours.

4. While the mollejas are marinating, prepare the coals asado style (see page 27).

5. Remove the mollejas from the marinade and rinse them with water, to prevent the yogurt from burning while grilling.

6. Put the mollejas over medium-hot coals and grill until a bit crispy and lightly browned on both sides, 10 to 12 minutes.

7. Simultaneously, grill the lemons until softened, turning and cooking for 2 to 3 minutes.

8. Once crisped and lightly browned, butterfly the mollejas, then squeeze one of the warmed lemons over the meat and grill for an additional 8 to 10 minutes, until they become crispy on all sides but do not burn.

9. Once the mollejas are cooked, remove them from the heat and slice them into thin strips, as you would for fajitas.

10. Squeeze the remaining lemon over the meat and season with salt and pepper to taste.

11. Serve in a fresh flour tortilla with ripe avocado slices and zesty pico de gallo. Add onions and tomatoes, grilled asado style, for even more layers of flavor and texture, if desired.

Mr. Adolph Trevino and Grandpa Raul at the sausage plant with a batch of handmade, all-beef "hot gut" sausage.

BEEF SAUSAGE

MAKES **3 DOZEN SAUSAGES, ⅓ POUND EACH (SIZE WILL DEPEND ON HOW FULL THE SAUSAGE IS. THE CASING CAN EXPAND TO FIT MORE.)**

Beef sausage, or Texas hot gut, is a huge player in the state's culture and foods. Originally influenced by several immigrant cultures, from Czech to German and Mexican, it started appearing on menus across Texas in the late 1800s. In the 1940s, my grandfather worked as a butcher in Luling's Bob Davis Locker Processing Plant, which is where he learned to make sausage, from the source. He added cayenne and smoked the sausages over mesquite coals for 3 to 4 hours. There were other variations at the time; for example, Czech sausage had garlic, while German did not. He made it German style, without garlic. My grandfather and Uncle Adolph started selling their sausage in 1950, and we've used the same beef sausage recipe since 1955.

They used to distribute their sausage, in the mid-1960s to early '70s, to restaurants on the east and west sides of San Antonio. In those years, the restaurant regulations weren't as strict and there was more of a free market. We could sell sausage wholesale to local grocery stores from Fort Worth to Corpus Christi. On Allende Street in Seguin, there used to be a "sausage plant" staffed only by Davila's employees. The fire needed for the cooking process was underneath the building, with steps leading down to it. As a three- or four-year-old, I thought it was like looking down the steps to hell. The smoke came up the stairs and there were flames inside. My father remembers it looked like a dungeon.

By 1973, the sausage plant was no longer needed because Grandpa Davila moved his operation to a much larger building across the street. (The original Davila's location was a shack across from the current location.) The handcrafted aspect of the sausage that began when Grandpa Davila worked as a butcher remains in place to this day. It's a three-day process: mix the meat, stuff the casings, and smoke them. It takes teamwork and passion, and love goes into every labor-intensive link.

Eat these with pickles, onions, sausage, bread, and jalapeños . . . and sauce. Put them in rice, on fries, in chili, or even with eggs for breakfast.

continued

4 yards pork tripe (hog intestine casings)

6 pounds beef cheek, cut into chunks

6 pounds brisket, cut into chunks

1¼ cups dried milk powder (as a binder)

1½ tablespoons cayenne pepper

⅓ cup freshly ground black pepper

⅓ cup salt

¼ cup pink curing salt

4 cups water

TOOLS:

Cotton twine

Metal rod for your smoker

Hand grinder or motorized grinder

Hand or hydraulic sausage stuffer

1. One day to 2 hours before: Soak the hog casings, to reconstitute them, for at least an hour.

2. Spread out the casings and cut them into 10-inch lengths.

3. Cut 8-inch pieces of twine, one per cut section of casing.

4. Tie a piece of twine on one end of each casing to close it and leave the other end open.

5. Set the tied casings aside, soaking in water.

6. One hour before: Prepare the smoker for indirect cooking. The grate of your smoker will need to be removed and replaced with a single metal rod, laid right across the grill for the sausages to be strung on.

7. Grind the meat into chili-size pieces.

8. Mix the milk powder, cayenne, black pepper, salt, and pink curing salt in a large bowl along with the water, making a slurry. Mix the slurry with the ground meat.

9. Change the grinder plate to hamburger size. Grind all the seasoned meat.

10. Put the open end of a length of casing on the nozzle of the sausage stuffer and fill the casing to 1½-inch-diameter thick, leaving 1½ inches of casing empty at the open end, so

MEAT-GRINDING TIPS

If the meat is too cold (or frozen), it'll get stuck in the grinder. If it is too hot, it'll turn into mush. You want it to be between 40° and 60°F.

When cutting and breaking down the meat to grind, make sure that the size of the pieces accommodates your grinder's hole. Ideally, the meat will be two-thirds the size of the hole, so that it does not get stuck or come out the wrong size.

that you're able to tie it to the other end, to make it a sausage ring. Continue until all the casings are filled and tied.

11. Smoke the sausages until the casings are firm to the touch and crisp, and the sausage is a smoky, candy-apple red, 2½ to 3 hours. The fat (the white specks) needs to be almost all cooked away. Serve!

BEEF FAJITAS

What we know as beef fajitas today is a cousin of beef *arrachera*, a dish that some believe originated with the vaqueros driving their herds to South Texas in the 1930s. The American counterpart frequently has a plethora of ingredients used to break down this typically tough cut of meat. This version contains few ingredients and is meant to be fully cooked, but not well done. It is ideal at medium (with a little pink). Using beer as part of the marinade indicates up front what this dish is tailored and made for—parties, weddings, graduations, and beyond.

10 pounds skirt steak

2 (12-ounce) bottles Modelo Light

½ cup fresh lemon juice (from 4 to 5 lemons)

2 tablespoons olive oil

2 tablespoons freshly ground black pepper

¼ cup salt

1 tablespoon garlic powder

2 red bell peppers

2 green bell peppers

2 yellow bell peppers

4 tomatoes

8 green onions

1 large white onion, cut into 1-inch disks

6 jalapeños

30 Flour Tortillas (page 161)

Sliced avocado and Pico de Gallo (page 183) for serving

Fire-Roasted Tomato, Onion, and Serrano Salsa (page 174)

1. Trim the skirt steak of any excess fat and remove the tough membrane. Score the meat diagonally with ½-inch-deep cuts. This allows for the marinade to fully penetrate.

2. Combine the beer, lemon juice, olive oil, black pepper, salt, and garlic powder in a nonreactive pan (or for best results, in a Cryovac vacuum bag or a resealable plastic bag). Reserve 1 cup of marinade for basting later on. Put the steak in the bag with the marinade. Refrigerate and allow it to marinate for 2 hours.

3. Two hours before you'd like to start cooking, prepare the fire asado style (see page 27). The cooking should be over medium-heat coals.

4. Char the bell peppers over the open flame, turning until blackened on all sides.

5. Put the peppers in a resealable plastic bag to steam for 10 minutes, then peel off the skin and remove the seeds. Cut into thick strips (*rajas*). Set aside.

6. Take the meat out of the refrigerator and remove it from the marinade. Allow the meat to come to room temperature, about 30 minutes.

continued

7. Put the meat on the grill. Turn every 3 to 5 minutes and baste it with the reserved marinade each time you turn. Continue this process until cooked to medium, 40 to 45 minutes (turning about 8 times). Be careful to control flare-ups.

8. Remove the meat from the fire and allow it to rest for 10 to 12 minutes before slicing into thin strips across the grain.

9. Meanwhile, the grill the tomatoes, green onions, onion, and jalapeño.

10. Serve the steak with the grilled onions, roasted peppers, sliced tomatoes, thinly sliced jalapeños, and pillowy, freshly made tortillas. Top with avocado, pico de gallo, and Fire-Roasted Tomato, Onion, and Serrano Salsa.

LENGUA DE RES (SMOKED BEEF TONGUE)

SERVES 6 TO 8; MAKES 12 TACOS   PREP TIME: 5 MINUTES   COOK TIME: 6 HOURS

When I was growing up, the aroma of this weekend treat permeated our home as we did our Saturday chores. I remember watching my mom prepare it and thinking how unappetizing it seemed to eat tongue, yet how surprisingly happy I was to sit down to this delicious meal after a long day of work. It is one of the best meals we would have as a family. Simmering the meat in beer, garlic, and spices means it's no longer tough or gamey, just tender and full of good flavors.

1 (2- to 3-pound) beef tongue

2 (16-ounce) bottles Negra Modelo beer

6 garlic cloves

6 bay leaves

1 tablespoon salt

1 tablespoon Davila's Signature BBQ Rub (page 43)

1 tablespoon olive oil

3 tomatoes, sliced into strips

¼ large yellow onion, sliced into strips

Twelve 6- to 8-inch flour tortillas

Tomatillo Salsa (page 179) for serving

1. Put the tongue in a large saucepan, with water to cover, over medium heat. Stir in the beer, garlic, bay leaves, and salt. Bring to a medium simmer and cook until the meat is no longer red, more gray, and begins to become tender, 2½ to 3 hours.

2. Preheat the smoker to 275°F.

3. Remove the tongue from the saucepan and put it on a sheet of aluminum foil. Season it with Davila's BBQ Rub, then wrap the foil around it.

4. Put the wrapped meat in the smoker to cook until thoroughly smoked and more tender to the touch, at 275°F for 3 hours.

5. Remove from the heat and allow it to cool, about 15 minutes.

6. Remove the membrane from the tongue by slicing it down the middle ¼-inch deep, flaying it open, and pulling it away. Dice the meat into ¾-inch cubes.

7. Heat the oil in a skillet over medium heat and cook the meat with the tomatoes and onion, stirring frequently, until the onion is translucent, 5 to 6 minutes.

8. Serve in fresh flour tortillas with Tomatillo Salsa.

TEXAS-STYLE BARBACOA

MAKES **6 TO 8 POUNDS OF COOKED MEAT**   PREP TIME: **4 HOURS, PLUS THE TIME TO DIG THE PIT**

COOK TIME: **6 TO 9 HOURS**

For thousands of years, cultures throughout the world have cooked food in the ground. From the Hawaiian Imu cooking to the North American clambake, these traditions were expressions of creativity and of necessity, facilitating an even, slow cooking of the food.

The origins of barbacoa are no different. Although today it's prepared using different methods, the concept of cooking a whole beef head in the ground with wood coals was known in the Aztec culture as *tatema*. Throughout Mexico and South Texas, barbacoa may refer to different meats and styles of preparation. In this case, I am referring to the process of slow cooking, overnight, a whole beef head in a pit in the ground, wrapped in maguey leaves.

We prepared this entire recipe in my backyard at the ranch, from harvesting the maguey leaves to digging the pit and gathering the mesquite. You can make it by simply cooking in a hole dug directly into the ground that's then been lined with rocks or firebricks or you can slide a barrel (or two large pipes, as we did) into a hole to make a more permanent in-ground barbecue.

To make whole-head barbacoa tacos, serve the meat in a tortilla and top with chopped onions and cilantro. Squeeze some lime or add Mama Davila's Salsa Picante (page 181) for a treat—after a lot of hard work!

10 to 12 maguey leaves

1 whole beef head, thoroughly rinsed

12 to 15 garlic cloves

½ cup salt

3 tablespoons chopped fresh parsley

TOOLS:

Shovel

Rocks or firebricks

Mesquite wood chunks

Chimney starter

Metal cable

TIP

You can buy a whole beef head from a local butcher or meat processor.

PREPARE THE PIT:

1. Dig a 36-inch-diameter hole 4 to 5 feet in the ground.

2. Line the bottom of the pit with rocks or firebricks.

3. Build the fire using large (6-by-18-inch) chunks of mesquite wood. Light the fire using hot coals from a chimney starter (see page 28). The wood needs to burn for 2½ to 3 hours, down to the coals, before it is time to place the beef head in the pit. (Having enough heat is key, as there's no putting the meat back or rebuilding the fire if it's undercooked!)

PREP THE MAGUEY LEAVES:

4. Prepare an open fire on a grill.

5. Use gloves when handling raw maguey leaves, as their juice is a natural skin irritant. Trim away the spines along the sides of each leaf. (Best to do this outside as it can get messy!)

6. Cook the maguey leaves on a grill or over hot coals until they are pliable and the liquid has been completely extracted, 10 to 15 minutes. You will hear them pop and sizzle.

COOK THE BEEF:

7. Using a paring knife, make incisions in the beef head and then stuff them with garlic cloves.

8. Use a large pot that has a top. Overlap the cooked maguey leaves vertically, so as to completely line the bottom and sides of the pot. The tips of the leaves may hang over or out of the rim.

9. Place the beef head inside the pot with the nose facing up. Fold over the maguey leaves to completely wrap the beef head.

10. Add 3 to 4 inches of water and then secure the lid to prevent steam from escaping. (You can tie it or weight it with a rock.)

continued

MAGUEY LEAVES are indigenous to South Texas, and you can find the spiky, thorny-edged plants most everywhere. The nectar inside each leaf has a distinctive tangy and citrusy flavor, similar to that of aloe vera but a bit peppery as well. That nectar drips down onto the vegetables cooking below the lamb and serves to flavor the vegetables in the *consomé*, a brothlike soup served alongside the meat. Agave, what tequila is made of, is the root of the maguey plant.

11. Use a metal cable to lower the pot into the pit in the ground. Make sure not to use rope as it could burn. Cover the hole thoroughly, so that no air can escape. I used a piece of sheet metal on top. Corrugated roof panels can also work. Do not use wood as the fire is too hot. Cover the metal top and the area surrounding the hole with dirt. Covering the hole will cut off the oxygen source to the fire, leaving only the heated rocks and the burning coals, which allows hot steam to cook the meat.

12. Steam until the meat falls off the bone, a process that should take 8 hours. Be sure to watch your timing. If the meat isn't fully cooked, the fire will no longer be hot enough to put it back in the ground and continue cooking.

13. Remove the meat from the bones then separate it by cuts: tongue, cheek, and so on, and serve, or slice and serve all the meats mixed together.

14. Reap the benefits of all your hard work.

WHOLE BBQ BORREGO FOR BARBACOA

SERVES **15 TO 25**   PREP TIME: **2½ TO 24 HOURS**   COOK TIME: **6 HOURS**

We think of barbecue as an all-American creation, dominated by beef and pork. But lamb, which is one of the least consumed types of meat in the United States, happens to be the most barbecued meat in the world, from the Middle East to Europe.

Upon coming to the New World, the Spanish adapted the local technique of cooking lamb by wrapping the meat tightly in maguey leaves, then roasting it in a pit dug into the ground. The heat of wood coals would steam the meat in the leaves for many hours, steeping it in the natural moisture from the maguey leaves and the meat itself. The term and technique then known as *barbacoa* is what we know as barbecue today.

In this recipe, we cook vegetables underneath the wrapped lamb. This method reaches back to the French technique of spitfire roasting over vegetables that allows the drippings from the meat to cook the vegetables. I sometimes use banana leaves instead of maguey because, aside from being hard to find, maguey have thorns and require the extra step of toasting them to become pliable. So, there you have it, a Mexican barbecue that showcases New World and French techniques.

1 (30-pound) dressed lamb (preferably 3 months old and grass fed)

3½ cups Adobo Marinade (recipe follows), or use store-bought from a Latin market

10 to 12 maguey leaves

3 medium red potatoes, cut into ½-inch cubes

2 medium carrots, peeled and cut into ½-inch cubes

1 medium white onion, halved and thinly sliced

2 garlic cloves, peeled and halved

1. Put the meat into a large, nonreactive dish. Pour the Adobo Marinade in to cover it completely, rubbing the mixture into the meat. Cover and refrigerate to marinate for at least 2 and up to 24 hours.

2. In the pit, about 30 minutes before cooking, prepare a charcoal fire, letting the coals burn until they are covered with a gray ash and are medium-hot. (Alternatively, preheat the oven to 275°F.) Remove the lamb roast from the refrigerator.

3. Cook the maguey leaves on the grill or over coals until they are pliable and the liquid has been extracted, 10 to 15 minutes. You will hear them pop and sizzle.

4. Combine the potatoes, carrots, onion, garlic, garbanzos, and epazote in a roasting pan large enough to hold the lamb. Put

1 cup cooked or canned garbanzo beans

1 large sprig epazote

2 handfuls of dried avocado leaves

Salt

¼ cup chopped fresh cilantro

TOOLS:

Cotton twine

the pan in the center of the grill grate. Pour water into the pan to about 2 inches from the top (6 to 8 cups). Put a V-shaped roasting rack into the watery vegetable mixture.

5. Sprinkle the avocado leaves over the top and bottom of the meat. Wrap the roast in the maguey leaves, tying it with twine.

6. Put the wrapped lamb on the roasting rack, at the bottom of the V—it will skim the surface of the water. Cover the pan tightly with aluminum foil. Cover the grill and cook, maintaining a moderately low temperature (275°F). The meat will easily pull off the bone after 6 hours (same cook time for the oven).

7. Unwrap the roast and, using a couple of meat forks or spatulas, put the roast on a heatproof platter lined with cooked maguey leaves. Reserve the liquid in the roasting pan. Discard any avocado leaves that cling to the meat and break the meat into large chunks. Sprinkle with salt, cover loosely with foil, and keep warm in a low oven.

8. Skim off the fat floating on the surface of the liquid in the roasting pan and discard. Season the broth with salt to taste, usually about ¾ teaspoon. Stir in the cilantro and ladle the broth into small, warmed soup cups. Serve the meat alongside the soup.

NOTE: Epazote is an herb that adds a strong oregano, fennel, and mint type of flavor profile to Mexican cooking. It can be hard to find it fresh, but you can often buy dried epazote in Latin markets, or online. Also available online, at Amazon, for example, are dried avocado leaves, which I encourage you to track down as there's no real substitute for the nutty hazelnut and anise flavor. Both of these herbs are thought to have a wide variety of medicinal qualities and are sometimes prepared as teas.

ADOBO MARINADE

MAKES ABOUT 3½ CUPS

PREP TIME: 5 MINUTES

COOK TIME: 20 MINUTES

10 dried guajillo chiles, stemmed and seeded

10 dried ancho chiles, stemmed and seeded

5 cups water

⅓ cup cider vinegar

1 large tomato, cut into quarters

½ cup coarsely chopped white onion

3 garlic cloves

1 tablespoon dried oregano

½ teaspoon ground cinnamon

½ teaspoon ground allspice

½ teaspoon freshly ground black pepper

5 whole cloves, stems removed

2½ teaspoons kosher salt

3 tablespoons vegetable oil

1. Heat a large skillet over medium heat. Toast the dried chile peppers for no more than 20 seconds per side, taking care not to burn them.

2. Put the chiles in a medium saucepan and add the water, put saucepan over medium heat, and cook until the peppers have softened and rehydrated, 12 to 15 minutes.

3. Transfer the peppers and 2 cups of the cooking liquid to a blender. (Discard the remaining liquid and rinse out the saucepan.) Add the vinegar, tomato, onion, garlic, oregano, cinnamon, allspice, black pepper, cloves, and salt; puree until smooth.

4. Heat the oil in the rinsed saucepan over medium heat for 1 to 2 minutes, then add the pureed marinade. Partially cover and cook, stirring once or twice, until the color darkens and the mixture thickens, 10 to 12 minutes.

TIP

If you need to use the oven method, add about 1½ teaspoons of liquid smoke to the Adobo Marinade.

CHILES IN BRIEF

Chipotle chiles are dried, smoked jalapeños. Their flavor is intense and smoky. The adobo sauce they're usually packed in consists of tomatoes, garlic, spices, and vinegar and is used to marinate meats and flavor chilis.

Ancho chile is a dried form of green poblano with a flavor profile that's a bit like tobacco. It makes a bright red, vibrant sauce.

Guajillo chile is used in the sauce base for tamales and also used in adobo sauce. They're rich tasting but not particularly spicy.

Serrano peppers have a sharper, stronger heat than their cousin the jalapeño, and are even more intense when roasted, as I often do.

Chiles de arbol are the hottest peppers I use. They start out green, then ripen to red. The redder they are, the more intense the heat.

BEEF JERKY

MAKES **40 TO 50 PIECES**   PREP TIME: **18 TO 20 MINUTES, PLUS 12 TO 15 HOURS TO MARINATE**

COOK TIME: **6 TO 8 HOURS**

Texas has a big outdoorsmen community, and many in that crowd are proud of their personal techniques for preparing and selling their own jerky and sausage. A small investment in a dehydrator can make a big difference when making your own jerky, but if you're not ready to purchase one, a practical alternative is to use the oven.

I like making jerky because the smell of the meat and the spices that fills the air reminds me of my grandfather. Plus, it's easy to make and a very convenient snack for on the go—whether you're driving cattle or a pickup truck.

2 pounds beef flank steak or eye of round, frozen for about an hour to make slicing it easier

½ cup water

¼ cup soy sauce

3 tablespoons Worcestershire sauce

1 teaspoon mesquite liquid smoke

2 tablespoons brown sugar

1 tablespoon fresh coriander seeds, crushed

2 teaspoons salt

1 teaspoon onion powder

1 teaspoon garlic powder

1 teaspoon chili powder

1 teaspoon freshly ground black pepper

½ teaspoon red pepper flakes

1. Cut the meat into thin slices, ¼- to ½-inch thick and 6- to 8-inches long, being sure to slice against the grain.

2. Mix together the water, soy sauce, Worcestershire sauce, liquid smoke, brown sugar, coriander seeds, salt, onion powder, garlic powder, chili powder, black pepper, and red pepper flakes in a large, nonreactive bowl or resealable plastic bag.

3. Add the meat and marinate in the refrigerator for 12 to 15 hours.

4. Remove the meat from the marinade and put into the cold smoker. Smoke until completely dry, 6 to 8 hours.

5. If using an oven, preheat the oven to 175°F. If using a dehydrator, follow the instructions on your machine.

6. Lay out the strips wire racks set on baking sheets if using the oven on dehydrator trays (or) and bake until dry and firm, flipping halfway through, for a total of 6 to 8 hours, depending on the thickness of the meat and heat or brand of dehydrator.

7. Remove the jerky and store in a sealed container or bag in the refrigerator for up to 1 month.

MESQUITE-SMOKED LAMB RIBS WITH CHIMICHURRI

SERVES 3 TO 4   PREP TIME: **12 TO 24 HOURS**   COOK TIME: **3 TO 3½ HOURS**

You'll rarely find lamb on barbecue menus in Texas and throughout the United States; in fact, the only state that can call lamb a barbecue "mainstay" is Kentucky. But at Davila's, barbecued lamb has been embraced by our customers for more than six decades. The origin of chimichurri sauce is unclear, but one theory is that the Basque settlers from Spain, who arrived in Argentina as early as the 19th century, named it. I enjoy these Old World flavors because the tang and bite of the sauce cuts through the fatty, smoky, savory ribs, and it goes well on any meat: beef, poultry, and/or fish.

¼ to ½ cup Davila's Signature BBQ Rub (page 43)

1 (2½- to 3½-pound) breast of lamb

Davila's Original BBQ Sauce (page 172) for serving

Adrian's Roasted Red Bell Pepper and Serrano Chimichurri Sauce (recipe follows) for serving

1. Rub the BBQ Rub thoroughly into the meat, covering all crevices of the lamb breast. Cover and refrigerate to marinate for 12 to 24 hours.

2. Thirty minutes before you want to cook, prepare a mesquite indirect fire in a barbecue pit or grill to achieve an even mix of smoke and heat, reaching 275°F (see page 30).

3. Put the lamb breast in the middle rack of your barbecue pit, over indirect heat. Cook until the meat is fork-tender, 3 to 3½ hours.

4. Remove the lamb breast from the pit and allow to rest for 25 to 30 minutes before slicing the ribs into individual portions.

5. Serve with Davila's Original BBQ Sauce and my special serrano chimichurri sauce.

ADRIAN'S ROASTED RED BELL PEPPER AND SERRANO CHIMICHURRI SAUCE

MAKES 3 CUPS

1 red bell pepper, roasted and then peeled

3 to 4 serrano peppers, roasted and then peeled

1 cup olive oil

I cup packed chopped fresh flat-leaf parsley

½ cup red wine vinegar

½ cup chopped fresh cilantro

¼ cup chopped fresh basil

6 sprigs fresh thyme

1½ teaspoons minced garlic

1 teaspoon salt

1 teaspoon ground cumin

1. Blend all the ingredients in a food processor until smooth, then transfer the mixture to a bowl.

2. Cover and let stand at room temperature until serving. The sauce can be made up to 2 hours ahead.

WHOLE PIG ASADO STYLE

SERVES **ABOUT 25**   PREP TIME: **3 DAYS**   COOK TIME: **6 HOURS**

Whole-animal cooking, whether in the ground over coals and rocks, above the ground, wrapped in coals, over coals in smoke, or smoked with heat, is a big event. The aromas and smells and eye candy lock us in, in a primal sense. What's more, the anticipation increases all day long as the meat is turned and marinated and the fire is kept going just right. From a purely practical standpoint, roasting a whole pig is a low-maintenance feast that feeds large numbers. And whether cooked on a spit, turned over or under a flame, or in a self-made pit in the ground, a pig roast is a tradition found all over the world: at Filipino Christmas celebrations; special occasions in Cuba; and in China, where a pig is sacrificed to ward off evils in return for success. Reaching back into history, the Saxons of Western Europe made a roasted wild boar the centerpiece of the meal at Yuletide; and in America, the tradition is prominent in the South, where it is closely linked to barbecue.

The specific recipes often come down to what's available, whether it's the wood for the rotisserie fire in Europe or, as in my case, the chiles found in Mexico. Cubans often don't season the meat at all before cooking because they believe the heat burns the seasoning off; they season it afterward with achiote and salt. Puerto Rican style uses lots of citrus.

We cook pigs whole most often when we're catering large gatherings. My favorite cooking method is Cuban style, which is directly over coals. It seems to take a bit more finesse than just using the smoker, and the hot flame renders the fat more, as opposed to the low and slow method of smoking. I feel slow smoking lets the pork sit in its fat too much and it becomes a bit oily. When it is made asado style, the result is less fatty, yet the meat still retains a very tender texture.

continued

1 (50- to 60-pound) pig, frozen

20 pounds ice

THE PIG PRIMER:

1. Three days before you want to cook, select a pig in the 50- to 60-pound range. The best pigs for roasting on a spit are under 90 pounds. At this weight, the meat will be extremely gelatinous and the flesh practically melts. Larger, older pigs have tougher fat, which can be more dry. You can buy a whole pig at your local butcher. The pig's head and feet will be attached. Ask for the pig to be butterflied with all internal organs removed, a.k.a. dressed.

2. A whole 50-pound pig will not fit in the average refrigerator to defrost, so how do we do this? We pull out a large, heavy-duty, "Texas-size" cooler. Make sure that the pig is laid on its side inside the cooler. It will take one day in the cooler for the whole pig to start to defrost.

3. After two days, the pig will begin to thaw. On this day, place 20 pounds of ice inside the chest/abdomen cavity of the pig.

4. On the third day, the pig will be thawed enough to start seasoning; the rub instructions follow. Make sure that the internal temperature of the pig does not exceed 40°F.

5. Build the fire: Use briquettes for this recipe, as I find that hardwood burns too fast and too hot, making it difficult to obtain an even, slow roast–level of heat. You will need 1 pound of coals per 10 pounds of pig. But make sure to have an extra 25 pounds on hand—you wouldn't want to run out of coals in the middle of your roasting process.

TOOL NOTES:

1. The fire for the pig is typically made in a metal oil barrel, a 55-gallon drum that's been split in half, so that it's about 24 by 32 inches, and filled with hardwood charcoal briquettes.

2. Use a chimney starter. It's the easiest way to get those coals lit!

3. The spit (source it online or have it custom made) is a tried-and-true way of cooking by exposing the whole animal to the heat in a spread-open manner.

4. Have ready baling wire, to secure the pig to the spit.

5. Grab a long set of tongs to arrange the coals under the roasting pig.

THE RUB:

4 cups olive oil

1½ cups salt

1½ cups freshly ground black
pepper

½ cup crushed garlic

¼ cup chopped fresh oregano

PREPARING THE PIG:

1. Combine the olive oil, salt, pepper, garlic, and oregano in a large bowl. Mix well until it forms a paste.

2. Rub only the inside cavity of the pig completely with the paste. (Rubbing the outside of the pig with the paste will make it scorch and burn.)

3. One of the most important steps in preparing your pig is securing it to the spit. This pig will be heavy. If it is not well secured, it will make for a sloppy roast. There are a few ways to secure the pig to the spit; I will address the "commercial spit" method as it is the most straightforward. Find a large, clean surface on which to lay the pig flat. Secure the spine to the spit for best results. Slide the spikes into position around the pig's jowls and right into the rear end, and lock the pig on by tightening the screws. Use baling wire to secure the hooves to the secondary bar. Your pig will look as if it's standing upright when secured correctly.

4. Cooking the pig is one of the easiest parts of this recipe. All you will need to do is sit back and relax, and take turns constantly rotating that pig. You can purchase an electric spit that rotates on its own, which is even less work—but it's also less fun. Roast your pig for 4 to 6 hours. You will know it's cooked when the skin is crispy, crackly, and a mahogany color. Note: If the skin started to be crispy within the first hour, you will need to either move the coals lower or the pig higher, as it is cooking too quickly.

5. When serving the meat, some people have "choice" parts they prefer to eat, such as cheek, backstrap (tenderloin), and loin, all of which are commonly sought after. The organs are usually reserved for sausages, soups, and other delicacies.

PORK RIBS

SERVES **4 TO 6**   PREP TIME: **10 MINUTES, PLUS 12 TO 24 HOURS TO MARINATE**

COOK TIME: **2½ TO 3½ HOURS, DEPENDING ON SIZE OF RIBS**

They key to this recipe is to let the ribs cook long enough to fall off the bone, but not so long that they overcook and dry out—and if you undercook them, they'll be tough. The finesse is dialed in from the smoke. Your goal is a red smoke ring around the outside of the sweet pink pork meat.

1 (3- to 3½-pound) slab of ribs

¼ cup Davila's Signature BBQ Rub (page 43)

1. Season the ribs with Davila's BBQ Rub, rubbing them on all sides.

2. Marinate the ribs for 12 to 24 hours in the refrigerator.

3. Prep your grill to use the indirect-heat smoking method (see page 30).

4. Smoke the ribs until they are tender and the meat falls off the bone, 2½ to 3½ hours. You can tell when the ribs are done cooking when you pick it up from the middle of the slab. If it is not done it will bend a little bit, but when it is done, the slab should fold over.

SMOKED PULLED PORK

SERVES **10 TO 12**   PREP TIME: **20 MINUTES**   COOK TIME: **12 TO 14 HOURS**

This recipe is special to me because I made it on *The Kitchen*, for its 100th episode. There must have been 30 camera and production people on set, and all the chaos happening in such a small space made me really nervous. I felt honored to be there with top-caliber guests. It was one of the first times I felt part of the "cooking club world" beyond Seguin.

Different cultures have their own versions of this fatty cut of meat that requires a long period of slow cooking to break down muscle tissue and become butter-tender. There's the Mexican version called *carnitas*, Italian *porchetta*, and Cuban *ropa vieja*. In the United States, "pulled pork" is to eastern barbecue what brisket is to Texas barbecue. It's a regional thing, and there's a lot of that going on in barbecue in general. Now, as regional barbecue customs cross paths, new versions are bound to appear.

Our pulled pork boasts the influence of South Texas through the use of cola, particularly Dr Pepper. You'll find it's a very versatile dish. We serve it on a bun, in tortillas, and even over nachos. Any leftovers can be served over rice, or Cuban style with black beans and rice. Condiments and toppings are varied and vast, but our favorites are spicy pico de gallo or pickled vegetables.

1 tablespoon vegetable oil

1 (3- to 4-pound) bone-in pork shoulder

2 teaspoons salt

1 teaspoon freshly ground black pepper

1 teaspoon cayenne pepper

2 tablespoons prepared yellow mustard

½ cup light brown sugar

1 medium onion, chopped

1 teaspoon mesquite liquid smoke

1 (12-ounce) can Dr Pepper

12 sandwich buns

1. Preheat a smoker to 275°F.

2. Rub the oil over the pork, to cover completely. Season with the salt, black pepper, and cayenne.

3. Next, rub the mustard over the pork, followed by a generous layer of brown sugar.

4. Put the pork roast, onion, liquid smoke, and Dr Pepper in a shallow roasting pan. Cover the pan and place it over indirect heat in the smoker. Cook until the bone in the shoulder pulls out completely, easily, and cleanly, 12 to 14 hours.

5. Remove the pork from the smoker, reserving the cooking liquid. Using two forks, pull apart and shred the pork. Stir in the reserved cooking liquid.

6. To serve, portion ½ to 1 cup of pulled pork per bun.

PORK LOIN WITH MUSTARD SEED SAUCE

SERVES **12 TO 15**   PREP TIME: **8 TO 10 MINUTES PREP, PLUS 3 TO 12 HOURS TO MARINATE**

COOK TIME: **1½ TO 2 HOURS**

Juicy and lean, this versatile brined and smoked pork loin can be eaten in sandwiches or as a main dish. It's one of my go-to recipes for entertaining, as it serves a crowd and smokes up beautifully with almost no prep time or effort. You could go a lot of directions with the condiments, but here I've shared a mustard seed sauce that complements it perfectly.

1 (6- to 7-pound) whole center-cut pork loin

1 recipe Davila's Liquid Brine (recipe follows)

1 tablespoon freshly ground black pepper

Mustard Seed Sauce (recipe follows)

1. Thirty minutes before cooking, prepare the grill for indirect smoking (see page 30).

2. Cut the loin in half horizontally. Marinate the loin in Davila's Liquid Brine in a nonreactive pan for 12 hours in the refrigerator.

3. Season all sides of the loin with pepper, then smoke until the internal temperature reads 135° to 140°F, 1½ to 2 hours.

4. Transfer the pork loin to a pan and tent it with foil. Allow it to rest for 15 to 20 minutes. Note that the temperature will continue to rise.

5. Slice and serve with mustard seed sauce.

> **NOTE:** You can use smaller loins or even a tenderloin for this recipe. Just adjust the cook time accordingly. A 3- to 4-pound loin would take 45 minutes to an hour, for example.

DAVILA'S LIQUID BRINE

MAKES **ABOUT 1 GALLON**

PREP TIME: **5 MINUTES**

COOK TIME: **20 MINUTES**

1 gallon hot water

4 cups (2 pounds) sugar

1 cup (½ pound) salt

½ cup freshly ground black
pepper

4 bay leaves

Heat the water in a very large pot over medium-high heat and stir in the sugar until it dissolves. Stir in the salt, pepper, and bay leaves and cook for 20 minutes.

MUSTARD SEED SAUCE

MAKES **ABOUT 2¼ CUPS**

PREP TIME: **5 MINUTES**

COOK TIME: **10 MINUTES**

¾ cup dry white wine

¼ cup diced onion

3 tablespoons yellow mustard
seeds

1 cup heavy whipping cream

3 tablespoons whole-grain Dijon
mustard

1 teaspoon minced fresh
rosemary

1 teaspoon minced fresh parsley

Pinch of salt

Pinch of freshly ground black
pepper

1. Combine the wine, onion, and 4¼ teaspoons of the mustard seeds in a small saucepan over medium heat and bring to a simmer. Cook until the sauce reduces by half, allowing the alcohol to evaporate, about 2 minutes.

2. Whisk in the cream, remaining 4¾ teaspoons of mustard seeds, and the Dijon mustard, rosemary, and parsley, raise the heat to medium-high, and cook, stirring frequently, until thickened and creamy, 5 to 6 minutes.

3. Whisk in the salt and pepper, to taste. Serve warm.

PUERCO EN CHILE COLORADO (PORK IN RED CHILE SAUCE)

MAKES **8 TO 10 SERVINGS**   PREP TIME: **10 MINUTES**   COOK TIME: **50 MINUTES**

The deep red color and bold flavors make this dish one of my favorites. It's a typical northern Mexican dish that's best with black beans and rice, served as a plate. I like to make a big pot and freeze some for later. Pork backbone (*espinazo de puerco*) is the bottom part of the pork loin. The bone adds body to the broth; that's why you use it in a stew. Plus, it's a little cheaper.

4 ounces guajillo chiles

⅓ pound tomatillos

½ cup manteca (lard) or vegetable oil

5 pounds pork backbone

½ large yellow onion, sliced

2 teaspoons salt

½ teaspoon ground cumin

3 garlic cloves

Cooked white rice for serving

OUTSIDE METHOD:

1. Prepare a fire asado style (see page 27).

2. Roast the guajillo chile pods directly on the fire embers for 3 to 4 seconds each, turning them once. This reconstitutes them and makes them plump up.

3. Using the same method, char the tomatillos for 5 to 7 minutes, turning them a few times, until blackened. Set aside.

INDOOR METHOD:

Alternatively, cook the chile pods in a cast-iron skillet over medium-high heat for about 10 seconds, or until they begin to fill with air and plump up. Then cook the tomatillos in the skillet, turning until charred.

COOK THE PORK:

4. On the stovetop, melt the manteca in a braising pan over medium heat. Add the pork, onion, and 1 teaspoon of the salt. Sauté until the pork is browned, 15 to 20 minutes. Lower the heat to a simmer.

continued

5. Combine the chiles with seeds, tomatillos, cumin, the remaining teaspoon of salt, and the garlic in a blender. Blend on high speed for 4 to 5 minutes, until completely smooth.

6. Raise the heat under the braising pan to medium. Stir the chile mixture into the pork and onion.

7. Cook until the pork easily falls off the bone when poked with a fork, 15 to 20 minutes.

8. Serve over white rice as a main dish.

SMOKED HAM WITH DAVILA'S BBQ SAUCE GLAZE

SERVES **8 TO 12**   PREP TIME: **5 TO 10 MINUTES**

COOK TIME: **APPROXIMATELY 15 TO 20 MINUTES PER POUND OF HAM**

On South Texas tables during the holidays, you will often see a traditional Anglo-American ham alongside tamales and chili con carne. This assortment represents the diversity and multiculturalism of the region, in both our population and our cuisine. I smoke my version of holiday ham, using our rub, and then create a glaze with our barbecue sauce that beautifully penetrates the meat. It's a slightly more savory take on an often very sweet flavor profile, and provides a good-looking centerpiece for the table. I like to serve this with sweet potatoes; see my Camotes over Coals (page 155).

1 (7- to 10-pound) bone-in, fresh uncooked ham

¾ cup Davila's Signature BBQ Rub (page 43)

1½ cups prepared yellow mustard

2 cups Davila's Original BBQ Sauce (page 172)

¼ cup honey

1. Prepare the smoker for indirect heat at 275°F (see page 30).

2. Score the ham ½-inch deep vertically and horizontally.

3. Rub the rub all over ham, including the flat side.

4. Put the ham in the smoker at 275°F, adding wood as needed to maintain the temperature. Cook until the juices start to run, about 1 hour.

5. Remove the ham from the smoker and rub the mustard over the ham. Cook until the mustard has formed a crusty layer, an additional 1½ hours. Remove the ham from the smoker.

6. Stir together the Davila BBQ sauce and the honey in a medium bowl.

7. Return the ham to the smoker with the thickest/fattest side up. Brush 1 to 2 cups of the sauce mixture over the ham, evenly covering all sides. Cook for an additional 30 to 45 minutes, until the ham reaches an internal temperature of 145°F. Do not allow the internal temperature to exceed 160°F. Be sure that the thermometer probe does not touch the bone, only

continued

the thickest part of the meat, or you could end up with a false temperature reading.

8. Transfer the ham to a large serving tray or cutting board, and present whole in the middle of the table. Serve one slice at time.

MORCILLA (SPANISH BLOOD SAUSAGE)

MAKES **24 TO 30 PIECES; SERVES 10 TO 12**   PREP TIME: **15 TO 20 MINUTES**

COOK TIME: **30 TO 40 MINUTES**

Originating in Spain, this recipe has roots as one of the very first sausage recipes, and is still found in France, Italy, and Spain. My first encounter with *morcilla* was deep in the Andes Mountains of Colombia, at a place called Villa de Leiba, where this sausage is served at open-air, roadside kiosks, sliced and served with crackers. The name intimidated me at first, but once I got over that, I found the sausage to be very tasty, with a strong iron flavor. It might be a lot of work, but it's worth the effort. You can buy the pork blood from your local butcher or order it online.

6 cups cooked white, medium-grain rice

6 cups pork blood

4 serrano peppers, stemmed and minced

4 garlic cloves, minced

4 teaspoons chopped fresh cilantro

4 parsley sprigs, chopped

4 bay leaves, crushed

2 teaspoons salt

1 teaspoon onion powder

1 teaspoon paprika

4 yards pork tripe (hog intestine casings)

TOOLS

Cotton twine

1. Stir together all the ingredients, except the tripe, in a large mixing bowl. Knead the mixture together by hand.

2. Morcilla is often cut and pan-fried, so I like to leave it in one long, circular sausage. Tie one end of the tripe shut and stuff. If you do not have a sausage stuffer, use a funnel. When filling the tripe, be sure to not overstuff the one long piece, to ensure that it closes properly and you can tie the other end.

3. Boil the sausage in a large stockpot until it has hardened, 25 to 30 minutes. Drain the water and allow the sausage to cool.

4. After the sausage has cooled, you can wrap it in butcher paper and freeze it. Frozen morcilla will last for 6 months. Or, if you're ready to serve it, slice the sausage into 1-inch-thick rounds and cook in a skillet over medium heat, stirring to achieve a crisp texture, 5 minutes.

CHICHARRONES EN SALSA VERDE

SERVES **6 TO 8**   PREP TIME: **5 TO 10 MINUTES**   COOK TIME: **25 TO 30 MINUTES**

Chicharrones (pork belly) are one of the true identifying foods of the Mexican culture, found border to border. They're best when you flavor them in some way. I serve them with salsa verde, which lends a tangy, bright, and acidic flavor, but they can take on any flavor you like. This version is typically *suave* (soft), though some people prefer them *tostadito* (crispy). Although this dish is high in calories, it is also high in protein and makes for an energizing, robust choice for breakfast.

1 pound tomatillos

4 serrano peppers

5 sprigs cilantro

1 garlic clove

1 teaspoon salt

4 cups water

1 tablespoon manteca (lard) or vegetable oil

½ large white onion, sliced

½ pound fried chicharrones

Cooked rice and black beans or corn tortillas for serving

1. Put the tomatillos and peppers in a medium saucepan. Add water to cover and cook over medium heat until the tomatillos are soft, 10 to 12 minutes.

2. With a slotted spoon, remove the peppers and tomatillos from the saucepan and transfer them to a blender. Discard the water.

3. Add the cilantro, garlic, salt, and 4 cups of fresh water to the blender. Blend until smooth.

4. Melt the manteca in a medium saucepan over medium-high heat. Add the onions and cook, stirring, until translucent, 2 to 3 minutes. Stir the blended tomatillo mixture into the onion, then add the chicharrones and simmer, allowing the chicharrones to absorb some of the sauce, 12 to 15 minutes.

5. Serve over rice and black beans or perfectly nestled in a corn tortilla.

NOTE: Chicharrones (pork belly, similar to cracklings) are available in Latin markets or the meat section of the grocery store.

MOLE DE OLLA CON PUERCO

MAKES 6 TO 8 SERVINGS   PREP TIME: **20 MINUTES**   COOK TIME: **1 HOUR 15 MINUTES**

Most moles are much more complicated than this one, as they usually use an enormous amount of ingredients. One look at the recipe and you figure you're going to be cooking for days. This mole features red chiles, and while not as labor intensive, it is still satisfying, meaty, and boasts a variety of vegetables for added texture and color.

3 pounds pork spine (it comes in 2- to 3-inch chunks)

¼ pound guajillo chiles

4 garlic cloves

1 tablespoon salt

2¼ teaspoons ground cumin

2 chayotes, cut into 1½-inch cubes

1 head broccoli, cut into florets

1 head cauliflower, cut into florets

1 zucchini, cut into 1½-inch cubes

¼ pound fresh green beans

½ large russet potato, cut into 1½-inch cubes

½ carrot, cut into 1½-inch cubes

1 sprig epazote, chopped

1. Bring 2 gallons of water to a boil. Boil the pork until no longer pink, 30 to 45 minutes.

2. While the pork is boiling, make the chile sauce mixture: combine 1 cup of the boiling water from the pork and the chiles, 3 of the garlic cloves, and the salt and cumin in a blender and blend until smooth.

3. Add the chile mixture to the boiling pork, then add the chayotes, broccoli, cauliflower, zucchini, green beans, potato, carrot, and remaining garlic clove to the pot and cook at a simmer, lowering the heat as necessary, until the potato is soft, 25 to 30 minutes.

4. Stir in the epazote. Serve in a bowl—this is a meal in itself.

WHOLE MESQUITE-SMOKED CHICKEN

SERVES 3 TO 4   **PREP TIME: 5 MINUTES, PLUS 12 TO 24 HOURS TO MARINATE**

COOK TIME: 2¹/₂ TO 3¹/₂ HOURS

Chicken is not featured in many barbecue joints in Texas, but at *quinceañeras*, weddings, and family reunions, it's always on the menu. This recipe walks the line with a good balance of juicy asado-style cooking and just enough smoke to provide the flavors of indirect cooking. I prefer smoking chicken with mesquite wood because it allows the delicate flavor of the meat and seasonings to come through with a less powerful smoky aroma. It burns quicker and hotter than other woods. Note that the chicken will crisp and turn a golden color, not the dark brown charred color produced by smoking with fruitwood.

I've been told that our barbecued chicken is the best around . . .

1 (3- to 3½-pound) whole chicken (giblets removed), split

1 tablespoon Davila's Signature BBQ Rub (page 43)

TOOLS:

Mesquite wood or mesquite charcoal

1. Rub all parts of the chicken thoroughly with Davila's BBQ rub, then place it in the refrigerator and allow to marinate overnight (12 to 24 hours).

2. Remove the chicken from the refrigerator 1 hour prior to cooking.

3. Thirty minutes before cooking, prepare to cook by lighting the smoker with indirect heat, until it reaches 275°F (see page 30). If a smoker is unavailable, use a grill: Light one end of the grill and place the chicken on the opposite side so it does not have direct contact with the heat, then proceed as follows.

4. Put the whole chicken in your smoker, skin side down, then close the lid. Leave the vents on your smoker at least a quarter of a turn open. After approximately 1 hour, flip the chicken so that the skin side is up. Check the temperature of the smoker

continued

to ensure the chicken is cooking correctly. Add more wood as needed to maintain 275°F.

5. The chicken is fully cooked when internal temperature reaches 165°F. Total cooking time will vary between 2½ and 3½ hours, depending on the size.

6. Wait 15 minutes before carving and serving.

CHICKEN FAJITAS

MAKES **24 TACOS, OR 10 TO 12 SERVINGS**   PREP TIME: **15 TO 20 MINUTES, PLUS 4 TO 6 HOURS TO MARINATE**   COOK TIME: **15 MINUTES DIRECT METHOD, 75 TO 90 MINUTES SMOKING METHOD**

In tacos, salads, or as a main dish, this South Texas staple has become mainstream American and can be found coast to coast, from Times Square to San Antonio to Hollywood. Most recipes use chicken breast, but I like to use chicken thighs because the meat doesn't dry out as easily.

1 cup fresh Valencia orange juice (about 3 to 4 oranges)

2 tablespoons salt

1 tablespoon dried oregano

1 tablespoon ground cumin

1 tablespoon garlic powder

1 teaspoon paprika

1 teaspoon crushed red pepper flakes

1 teaspoon onion powder

3 to 4 pounds boneless, skinless chicken thighs

¼ cup vegetable oil

2 red bell peppers

2 green bell peppers

2 yellow bell peppers

1 large white onion, cut into 1-inch-thick disks

24 flour or corn tortillas

Grated Cheddar, sour cream, Pico de Gallo (page 183), and avocado slices for serving

1. Combine the orange juice, salt, oregano, cumin, garlic powder, paprika, red pepper flakes, and onion powder in a resealable plastic bag or nonreactive dish. Marinate the chicken, covered in the refrigerator, in this mixture for 3 to 4 hours, but no more than 6 hours because the acidity of the orange juice will begin to cook the chicken.

2. Thirty minutes before cooking, prepare an asado-style fire (see page 27). Brush the chicken with oil, then put it directly on the grill, cooking for about 15 minutes, turning as needed.

3. Meanwhile, char the bell peppers, asado style, over the open flame, turning until blackened on all sides. Put them in a resealable plastic bag to steam for 10 minutes, then peel off the skin and remove the seeds. Set aside.

4. Grill the onion slices until charred and soft, 6 to 8 minutes, turning frequently.

5. Remove chicken and onion from the grill and allow the chicken to rest for 10 minutes.

6. Slice the cooked onion and peppers into strips.

7. Slice the chicken into strips 2½- to 3-inches long and ¼-inch wide.

8. Mix the chicken, onion, and peppers together and serve with freshly warmed tortillas, Cheddar, sour cream, pico de gallo, and avocado slices.

SMOKED CHICKEN FAJITAS

For a dose of mesquite flavor in your fajitas, preheat the smoker to 275°F to smoke indirectly (see page 30). Smoke the chicken for 75 to 90 minutes.

TINGA DE POLLO

SERVES **3 TO 4**   PREP TIME: **30 MINUTES**   COOK TIME: **1½ HOURS**

Created originally in the state of Guanajuato, this dish has achieved soul food status in Mexico. It's a traditional, homemade, everyday dish you can find in any kitchen across the country. The robust flavors of this dish include a smoky and spicy blend of tomato and chipotle sauce. You can serve this alongside rice and beans or on crisp corn tortillas as the very best tostadas, cooled down by such toppings as *crema*, *queso fresco*, lettuce, and avocado.

4 cups water

1 (3- to 4-pound) whole fryer chicken (giblets removed), cut into 8 pieces

2 yellow onions, 1 whole and 1 sliced

5 garlic cloves

2 teaspoons salt

1 teaspoon freshly ground black pepper

3 medium tomatoes, quartered

4 canned chipotle peppers with adobo sauce

½ cup manteca (lard) or vegetable oil

1. Combine 4 cups of water, the chicken, the whole onion, the garlic cloves, and the salt and pepper a large skillet. Bring to a simmer over medium-high heat and cook until the chicken is fully cooked and falling off the bone, 30 to 45 minutes. Remove from the heat and allow to cool.

2. Remove the chicken from the skillet, discarding the liquid, onion, and garlic. Reserve the skillet.

3. Cut the meat from the chicken, discarding the skin, and, using two forks, shred the chicken.

4. Grind the tomatoes and chipotle peppers on a molcajete until smooth. Alternatively, pulse them in a blender until smooth.

5. Over medium heat, melt the manteca in the skillet used for the chicken. Add the onion and the tomato mixture and cook, stirring, until the onion is translucent, 6 to 7 minutes.

6. Add the chicken back to the skillet and simmer over low heat, allowing chicken to absorb the sauce and its flavors, 15 to 20 minutes. Serve as desired (see headnote).

NOTE: A molcajete is a type of mortar and pestle made from volcanic rock, used for grinding food in Mexico.

CALABACITA CON POLLO (SQUASH WITH CHICKEN)

SERVES **4 TO 6**   PREP TIME: **10 TO 15 MINUTES**   COOK TIME: **20 TO 30 MINUTES**

The use of squash is prevalent in Mexican culinary traditions. Over the years, it has also become a staple in Texan cuisine. Coincidentally, if not strategically, this dish makes a very healthy meal. It is high in fiber, in contrast to many traditional starch-based Mexican dishes. Of course I find a way to get the added starch in there, as my favorite ways to serve it are over mashed potatoes or with flour tortillas, which I tear and dip into the soup until they are soft.

1 (3- to 3½-pound) whole chicken (giblets removed)

1½ teaspoons salt

1 teaspoon freshly ground black pepper

½ teaspoon ground cumin

½ cup manteca (lard) or vegetable oil

1 pound yellow or green squash, cut into ½-inch disks

½ large yellow onion, cut into ½-inch slices

4 large garlic cloves

2 cups chopped tomato

2 cups chicken broth

1 cup fresh corn kernels

Flour tortillas or mashed potatoes (optional) for serving

1. Cut the chicken into 10 equal pieces to ensure it will cook evenly. (Tip: Cut the breasts in half, so you have 2 wings, 2 thighs, 2 legs, and 4 breast pieces.)

2. Thoroughly season the chicken pieces with salt, pepper, and cumin.

3. Melt the manteca in a large skillet over medium-high heat. Add the chicken, lower the heat to medium, and cook until browned on all sides, turning as needed, for a total of 10 to 12 minutes.

4. Stir in the squash and onion and cook, stirring, until the onion is translucent, 5 to 6 minutes. Stir in the garlic and cook until fragrant, 1 to 2 minutes.

5. Add the tomato, chicken broth, and corn. Cover and lower the heat to a simmer. Cook until the ingredients blend to form a stewlike consistency, 8 to 10 minutes.

6. This dish can be served as a soup in a bowl with flour tortillas on the side, or as a stew spooned over mashed potatoes (or your choice of starch).

ARROZ CON POLLO (RICE WITH CHICKEN)

SERVES **4 TO 6**   PREP TIME: **15 MINUTES**   COOK TIME: **1 HOUR 15 MINUTES**

Arroz con pollo is a chicken and rice dish closely related to paella. In making paella, saffron is used to flavor the broth and color the rice yellow. Puerto Ricans claim to have created the first New World arroz con pollo. In their version, annatto, which is not traditionally used in Spain, replaces saffron, and they add tomatoes and peppers, which are native to the Americas.

My version has influences from both Puerto Rico and Spain but stays true to my South Texas and Mexican roots. I add cumin and garlic and eat it wrapped in tortillas and drizzled with my mama's red sauce. As a child, this dish was a personal favorite on cold weekends, as it simmered slowly on the stovetop. Although other recipes call for the chicken to be browned in the same pot as the rice, over time my mother found that boiling the chicken in a separate stockpot, prior to starting the rice, ensures a crispier outer skin and juicier meat.

1 gallon water

1 (3-pound) whole chicken (giblets removed), cut into 8 pieces

½ yellow onion, peeled

1 tablespoon ground annatto

1 garlic clove, peeled

2 tablespoons plus ¾ teaspoon kosher salt

2¼ teaspoons freshly ground black pepper

1 cup vegetable shortening or coconut oil

1 green bell pepper, seeded and diced

½ large sweet onion, diced

2 cups long-grain rice

1. Combine the water, chicken pieces, onion, annatto, garlic, 1½ tablespoons of the kosher salt, and 1½ teaspoons of the black pepper in a large stockpot over medium heat. Bring to a medium simmer, not a rolling boil, and cook until the chicken is halfway cooked, 20 to 25 minutes.

2. Remove the chicken from the liquid, reserving the broth.

3. Heat the shortening or oil in a large, straight-sided skillet over medium-high heat until hot but not smoking. Add the chicken and brown the skin, 4 to 6 minutes on each side.

4. Lower the heat to medium and add the green pepper and onion. Cook, stirring, until the vegetables are softened and fragrant, 6 to 7 minutes.

5. Add the rice and cook, stirring, until the rice begins to turn golden in color, 3 to 4 minutes.

6. Combine the reserved broth, tomato sauce, tomato, remaining ¾ teaspoon of black pepper and 2¼ teaspoons of the salt, and the garlic and cumin in a medium bowl.

1 cup tomato sauce

½ cup chopped tomato with seeds

1½ teaspoons minced fresh garlic

¾ teaspoon ground cumin

Corn or flour tortillas for serving

Mama Davila's Salsa Picante (see page 181)

7. Add the broth mixture to the skillet, making sure that the rice and chicken are covered and that the chicken is nestled into the rice. Bring to a boil, then lower the heat to medium-low and cover. Cook until the chicken is cooked through, the rice is tender, and most of the moisture is absorbed, about 35 minutes.

8. Let the skillet stand, covered, about 10 minutes before serving with warm corn or flour tortillas and Mama Davila's Salsa Picante.

NOTE: This recipe can easily be doubled using a very large skillet, or two skillets.

BRINED AND SMOKED WHOLE TURKEY

SERVES 12 TO 15   PREP TIME: 45 MINUTES, PLUS 12 TO 24 HOURS TO BRINE

COOK TIME: 4 HOURS 20 MINUTES

As a young boy, I would watch my grandfather use this technique, but I only rediscovered it while trying to solve a problem. A smoked turkey recipe I was working on kept coming out dry, so I delved into Old World methods for my more modern purpose. Before refrigeration existed, brining was developed to preserve meats longer. But brining also makes meat moister by hydrating the cells of the muscle tissue before cooking, via the process of osmosis, then by allowing the cells to hold on to the water while they are cooked. Brining can be used with all poultry and meats that tend to dry out, but it's not to be used with beef. You'll find it works wonders with fried chicken, chicken wings, and pork loin (see page 74).

Davila's Liquid Brine (see page 75)

1 (15- to 18-pound) turkey

Freshly ground black pepper

1. Place the brine in a very large pot over medium-high heat.

2. Place the turkey in the pot and soak it in the brine for 12 to 24 hours in the refrigerator.

3. Thirty minutes before cooking, prepare your grill for indirect-heat smoking (see page 30) or preheat a smoker to 275°F.

4. Remove the turkey from the brine and pat dry with a paper towel. Discard the brine and season the turkey with pepper.

5. Put the brined turkey in the smoker and cook until the internal temperature reaches 145°F, 3 to 4 hours.

6. Remove the turkey from the smoker and allow it to rest for 30 minutes before slicing and serving.

SOUTH TEXAS PEANUT BUTTER MOLE

SERVES 6 TO 8   **PREP TIME: 10 MINUTES**   **COOK TIME: 45 MINUTES**

My mom didn't have access to some of the traditional Mexican ingredients for her moles, so she improvised by using chili powder and peanut butter and sometimes prepared foods, such as canned tomatoes. You can think of it as an Americanized version of an "authentic mole," but in my world, this is a true South Texas mole—a home-cooked Tejano recipe, probably improved along the way by my grandmother. As in all good moles, the flavors meld together into, in this case, a beautiful caramel-colored sauce.

3 cups water

½ cup smooth peanut butter

2 tablespoons chili powder

1 tablespoon all-purpose flour

1 (3- to 4-pound) whole chicken (giblets removed), cut into 8 pieces

1 tablespoon salt

1 tablespoon freshly ground black pepper

2 tablespoons manteca (lard) or vegetable oil

2 garlic cloves, chopped

½ white onion, cut into ½-inch slices

Arroz Mexicano (page 156) or corn tortillas for serving

1. Thoroughly stir together 1 cup of the water and the peanut butter and chili powder in a medium bowl. Stir in the flour and set aside.

2. Season the chicken with the salt and pepper.

3. Melt the manteca in a large skillet over medium-low heat and cook the chicken until it begins to brown on both sides, for a total of 6 to 8 minutes.

4. Add the garlic and onion to the skillet and continue to cook, stirring, until onion begins to be translucent and the garlic is fragrant, an additional 3 to 4 minutes.

5. Stir in the prepared peanut butter mixture and the remaining 2 cups of water. Simmer until the sauce begins to thicken and the chicken is fully cooked, 20 to 25 minutes. The chicken should easily come off the bone.

6. Serve over Arroz Mexicano or with corn tortillas.

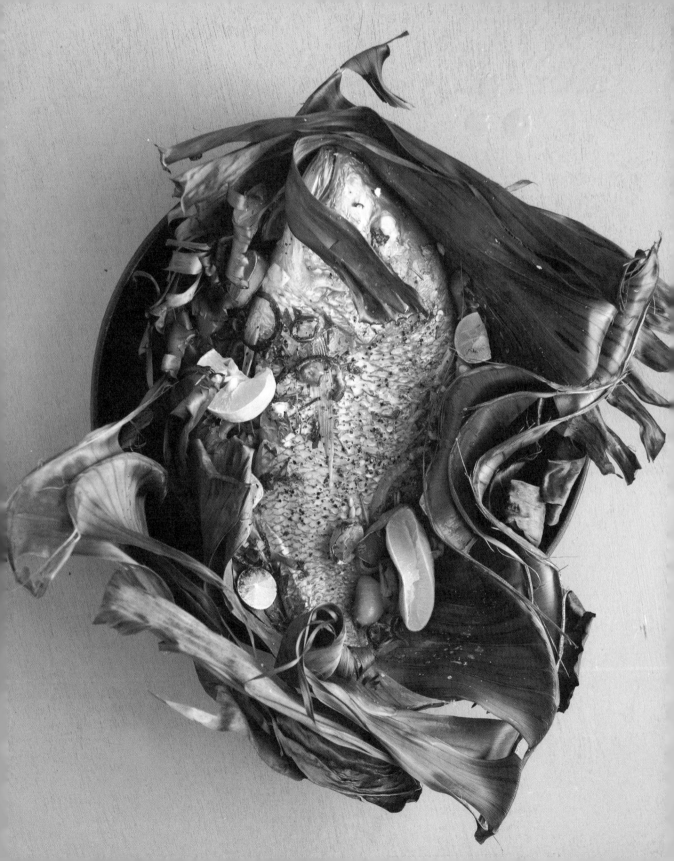

SEAFOOD

It's safe to say that vaqueros would not have had seafood as a big part of their diet, and they're not known for cooking the fish in rivers and lakes. But today in Seguin, we're blessed with fresh fish and seafood delivered to us straight from the waters of the Gulf of Mexico. The recipes here are rooted in my experiences as a caterer, my travels, and family events. I give them my twist on textures and flavors, always with a South Texas influence.

CAMARONES AL MOJO DE AJO (SHRIMP IN GARLIC SAUCE)

SERVES **4 TO 6**   PREP TIME: **10 MINUTES**   COOK TIME: **10 MINUTES**

My *BBQ Blitz* winning recipe for shrimp in garlic butter sauce features a whole head of garlic and chipotle peppers in adobo sauce, ensuring some full-flavored mojo. It's an easy, tasty dish that works as an appetizer over crackers, as a main dish served over rice and vegetables—and even as a taco filling.

1 large garlic head, cloves separated and peeled

8 tablespoons (1 stick) unsalted butter, at room temperature

2 tablespoons olive oil

½ white onion, cut into ½-inch cubes

3 to 4 chipotle peppers in adobo sauce, chopped

2 pounds (16/20 count) jumbo, shell-on, deveined shrimp

5 sprigs flat-leaf parsley, chopped

Juice of 1 lemon

1½ teaspoons salt

Freshly ground black pepper

1. Combine the garlic cloves, 4 tablespoons of the butter, and the olive oil in a blender. Blend on high speed until the ingredients are fully incorporated and the mixture appears smooth. Set aside.

2. Melt the remaining 4 tablespoons of butter in a medium cast-iron skillet over medium heat. Stir in the chopped onion and chipotle peppers and cook until they just start to turn transparent, about 1 minute.

3. Add the garlic butter mixture to the skillet and cook, stirring, until it begins to thicken, 2 to 3 minutes.

4. Add the shrimp to the skillet and cook, stirring frequently, until the shrimp become opaque, 3 to 4 minutes.

5. Stir in the parsley, lemon juice, salt, and pepper to taste. Continue to cook, stirring, as the sauce thickens further and the shrimp is cooked through, about 3 minutes. Be sure to not overcook the shrimp. Serve immediately.

MEXICAN SHRIMP AND OYSTER COCKTAIL

SERVES 25 AS AN APPETIZER, 10 TO 12 AS A MAIN COURSE   PREP TIME: 20 MINUTES

COOK TIME: 45 MINUTES (TO CHILL AND MARINATE)

This light dish of fresh seafood marinated in a pico de gallo is one of my father's signature party recipes. I know you're thinking, "What's with the orange soda?" Well, my dad's original recipe does not include it but I find it's often added to this dish in Mexico. There's a specific, slightly bubbly, citrus tang the soda adds. Serve this dish as an appetizer or meal, depending on how you pair it, with crackers or lettuce or over rice.

2 pounds jumbo shrimp, cooked, peeled and deveined

1 pound raw oysters

1 cup Clamato juice

2 cups ketchup

1 cup orange soda, such as Fanta

2 avocados, diced

2 tomatoes, diced

½ yellow onion, diced

⅓ cup chopped fresh cilantro

2 serrano peppers, seeded and diced

Juice of 2 limes

4 to 6 drops Tabasco, to taste

1 teaspoon salt, or to taste

1 teaspoon freshly ground black pepper, or to taste

1. Mix together the shrimp, oysters, and Clamato juice in a large mixing bowl.

2. Gently stir in the remaining ingredients.

3. Cover and chill in the refrigerator for 30 to 45 minutes before serving.

AGUACHILES DE CAMARONES (SHRIMP IN CHILI BROTH)

SERVES **8 TO 10**   PREP TIME: **10 MINUTES, PLUS 12 TO 15 MINUTES TO MARINATE**

In the tiny pueblo outside of Tulum, in Mexico's Yucatán Peninsula, I've eaten wonderfully fresh seafood prepared in this style, spiked with hyper-hot habanero peppers. I've toned it down here a little bit, using jalapeños instead. If you've had a long day suffering in the South Texas heat, this recipe is a quick treat. The balance of spice from the peppers, the zest of the lime sauce, and the crispness of the cucumber are what bring it all together. But a key to this recipe is the presentation, so be sure to butterfly and devein your shrimp. The acidity of the lime juice cooks the shrimp, and it's vital to get fresh (not frozen) shrimp to achieve the right texture and snap.

½ **bunch fresh cilantro**

1 **cup freshly squeezed lime juice (from about 8 limes)**

2 **to 3 jalapeño peppers**

2 **garlic cloves**

1 **teaspoon salt**

2 **cucumbers, thinly sliced**

1 **pound fresh (16/20 count) shrimp, butterflied and deveined**

½ **red onion, thinly sliced**

2 **avocados, peeled, pitted, and sliced**

Tostadas for serving

1. Combine the cilantro, lime juice, jalapeños, garlic, and salt in a blender. Blend until pureed.

2. Spread out the cucumber slices on one or two large, rimmed platters or shallow, nonreactive casserole dishes. Add a layer of shrimp. Top with red onion.

3. Pour the blended mixture over the top of the layered cucumber, shrimp and onion. Cover and allow it marinate for 10 to 15 minutes in the refrigerator.

4. Serve the cucumber, shrimp, onion, and slices of avocado stacked on top of tostadas.

SMOKED FRESH OYSTERS

SERVES **6 TO 8**   PREP TIME: **30 MINUTES, PLUS 24 HOURS**   COOK TIME: **2 HOURS**

"Barbecued smoked oysters" doesn't necessarily roll easily off the tongue, but the combined sweetness of the *piloncillo* and the bourbon produces a surprisingly clean-tasting, flavored brine.

INFUSED OIL:

1 cup extra-virgin olive oil

2 serrano peppers, thinly sliced into circles

4 garlic cloves, minced

Zest of 1 lemon

1 tablespoon chopped fresh cilantro

BRINE:

1 gallon water

½ cup Worcestershire sauce

1 cup bourbon (or Coca-Cola, for a nonalcoholic version)

1 cup piloncillo (Mexican unrefined brown sugar)

6 to 8 garlic cloves

1 tablespoon onion powder

½ teaspoon Tabasco

2 tablespoons salt

1 teaspoon freshly ground black pepper

OYSTERS:

48 freshly shucked oysters

Saltine crackers and Pico de Gallo (page 183) for serving

1. Make the spice-infused oil by combining all its ingredients in a bowl. Set aside in a covered container at room temperature.

2. Make the brine: Combine all the ingredients in a large, nonmetallic container. Mix until all the piloncillo dissolves.

3. Add the oysters to the brine and allow to marinate in the refrigerator, covered, for 24 hours.

4. One hour before you'd like to start cooking, prepare a smoker with indirect heat to 275°F (see page 30).

5. Remove the oysters from the brine. Rinse each oyster under cold water and arrange them on a grilling rack or in a vegetable or fish basket.

6. Smoke the oysters until they firm up and are slightly darker in color, about 2 hours.

7. Remove the oysters from the smoker and drizzle with the infused oil. Serve them over crackers, topped with pico de gallo for extra zest.

TEXAS GULF CEVICHE-STUFFED AVOCADOS

SERVES **6 AS A MAIN COURSE OR 12 AS AN APPETIZER**   PREP TIME: **15 TO 20 MINUTES**

COOK TIME: **1 HOUR**

I have served thousands of these at catering events as it is always one of our most popular requests. There's no wonder why, as it's a light and refreshing dish and our proximity to the Texas coast allows us to obtain the freshest fish and seafood. With a few simple ingredients you can create a colorful, beautifully presented, "all-in-one" meal. It's perfect for summer entertaining, too, because the fish cooks in the lime juice. You can serve it on its own or with saltine crackers.

½ **pound fresh Texas red snapper fillets, cut into ½-inch pieces**

½ **pound (26/30 count) fresh Texas Gulf brown shrimp, peeled and deveined**

⅓ **pound fresh bay scallops, cut into ½-inch cubes**

1 red onion, diced

1 tomato, diced

2 serrano peppers, seeded, deveined, and minced

¼ **cup chopped fresh cilantro, plus more for garnish**

¼ **teaspoon minced fresh oregano**

¼ **teaspoon salt**

¼ **teaspoon freshly ground black pepper**

Juice of 6 limes

6 avocados

1. Gently combine all the ingredients, except the lime juice and avocados, in a large, nonreactive bowl or dish.

2. Add the lime juice and allow to marinate for 1 hour, covered in the refrigerator.

3. When ready to serve, slice the avocados in half, discarding the pits, and scoop about 1½ tablespoons of the ceviche into each half. Garnish with cilantro and serve.

CARIBBEAN-STYLE WHOLE RED SNAPPER

SERVES **4**   PREP TIME: **2½ HOURS**   COOK TIME: **2 HOURS**

I discovered this dish while visiting coastal Colombia, where it is prepared with coconut milk and Asian flavors, such as ginger. My South Texas version replaces the spicy zing of ginger with that of jalapeño and cilantro. The yogurt, which I use as a substitute for the coconut milk, breaks down the enzymes of the fish, making the flesh more tender and less fishy in flavor. The colorful peppers and banana leaves create a beautiful presentation on the table.

1 cup plain Greek yogurt

½ cup olive oil

½ cup añejo tequila

¼ cup freshly squeezed lime juice (about 3 to 4 limes)

3 garlic cloves, minced

⅓ cup minced fresh cilantro

¼ cup (2 ounces) piloncillo

1 tablespoon salt

1 teaspoon freshly ground black pepper

1 red bell pepper, thinly sliced

1 yellow bell pepper, thinly sliced

1 (3½- to 4-pound) whole red snapper, scaled and cleaned

1 to 2 large banana leaves

Arroz Verde (page 157) for serving

TOOLS

Butcher twine

1. Stir together the yogurt, olive oil, tequila, lime juice, garlic, cilantro, piloncillo, salt, and pepper in a large, nonreactive dish. Rub the marinade over the entire fish.

2. Stuff the sliced peppers into the cavity of the fish and let the fish marinate, covered, in the refrigerator for 2 hours.

3. Heat the banana leaves on a skillet over medium heat for 2 to 3 minutes, turning every 30 to 45 seconds, until they become fully pliable. You should see some browning but no charring.

4. Two hours before you'd like to start cooking, prepare the grill for direct heat, asado style (see page 27).

5. Wrap the fish in the banana leaves much like you would a tamale (see page 120) and then tie it with butcher twine. Don't wrap the leaves too thickly or they won't transfer the heat well to cook the fish. Then wrap it in a layer of foil.

6. Grill the fish over direct medium-high heat for about 30 minutes, turning every 10 minutes.

7. Carefully cut down the center of the fish packet with a knife to remove and unwrap the fish while still hot, as you don't want the fish to continue to cook and become dry. For a creative presentation, plate the fish on the unwrapped banana leaves and serve with Arroz Verde.

NOTE: Using the banana leaves adds to the uniqueness of the recipe, Caribbean style. Banana leaves are now available at most Latin markets; however, you can also use parchment or foil.

GLAZED BARBECUED SALMON

SERVES 8 TO 10   PREP TIME: 5 TO 10 MINUTES, PLUS 14 TO 16 HOURS TO MARINATE   COOK TIME: 1 HOUR

The sweet flavor of the barbecue sauce and brown sugar balances the savory mesquite smoke in this dish. Salmon is ideal for dinner parties because of its presentation, flavor, and ease of preparation. And even better, you can serve this salmon hot or cold. Little effort and time go into its actual preparation. Yes, it does take a lot of time to marinate and cook, but it won't take away from your personal time with your guests. It tastes great served on its own as part of a dinner spread or as an appetizer on crackers garnished with diced tomatoes.

1 (3-pound) fresh salmon fillet

1 cup bourbon

1 cup dark brown sugar

½ cup Davila's Original BBQ Sauce (page 172)

1½ teaspoons kosher salt

½ teaspoon freshly ground black pepper

Saltine crackers and diced tomatoes for serving (optional)

NOTE: You'll need mesquite wood or charcoal for your smoker. When a smoker is unavailable, use a grill. Light one end of the grill and place the salmon on the opposite side so it does not have direct contact with the heat.

1. Place the salmon in a large glass or plastic dish, skin side down. Pour the bourbon on top, cover, and refrigerate. Allow to marinate for 2 to 4 hours.

2. Remove the salmon from the bourbon and discard the bourbon. Pat the salmon dry, using a paper towel, so that the sugar will stick properly. Rub the dark brown sugar all over the nonskin side of the salmon. Cover and refrigerate for 12 hours.

3. Remove the salmon from the refrigerator 1 hour prior to cooking. Rinse the salmon to remove the brown sugar and pat dry. Coat the salmon fillet with barbecue sauce and season with salt and pepper, set aside.

4. Thirty minutes before you'd like to begin cooking, prepare the grill for indirect heat (page 30) or the smoker until it reaches 275°F.

5. Place the salmon, skin side down, on the grill or in the smoker, then close the lid. Leave the vents on your smoker at least a quarter of a turn open.

6. Cook until the flesh starts to flake, 1 hour. Remove from the heat and serve immediately or allow to cool for 20 minutes.

STREET FOODS

The food in this chapter is directly influenced by the street foods in Mexico that I've enjoyed. There, as in other parts of the world, foods sold on the street are ingenious and inventive, creating exciting sights, sounds, and smells for the passersby. Nothing will get your attention like the whistle of the camote (sweet potato) carts, alongside taco stand cooks yelling, "Taco rico!" ("Delicious taco!"), or a simple corn dish in a cup that's comforting on a cold day. Street food has been elevated in recent years, reaching menus in fine dining restaurants, and chefs are creating their own twists.

As with the vaquero tradition, nose-to-tail cooking is abundant in the world of street tacos, and this simple food, once considered only for peasants, is now a sought-after delicacy. I've chosen to highlight some of my favorites here. These palm-size tacos are easily customizable, making them an efficient way to please a crowd. There's no need for sides, as the whole meal is folded up in the tortilla, perfect for walking and snacking, or a quick picnic on a bench. Similarly, tamales are well suited for the street. Wrapped up in the natural packaging of the steamed corn husk, they're prepped ahead of time and simply steamed for serving.

TACOS AL PASTOR (PINEAPPLE AND PORK)

MAKES **18 TO 20 MINI TACOS, OR 8 TO 10 SERVINGS**   PREP TIME: **15 TO 20 MINUTES, PLUS 12 HOURS TO MARINATE**   COOK TIME: **12 TO 15 MINUTES**

Al pastor ("the shepherd") is one of the most recognized street tacos in the Americas. The recipe has its roots in *trompo*, which is the meat you see being sliced from a rotating vertical skewer. Lebanese immigrants brought the shawarma style to Mexico, and in Greece you will find a similar recipe in a gyro. Both traditionally use lamb meat, hence the name, but in Mexico and South America al pastor is made with juicy pork.

1 pineapple, ½ cored and diced, ½ sliced into rounds ¾-inch thick

2 tomatoes, quartered

1 yellow onion, ½ roughly chopped, ½ sliced into rounds ¾-inch thick

1 cup fresh Mexican or Valencia orange juice (about 3 to 4 oranges)

3 guajillo chiles

2 ancho chiles

1 chipotle chile

3 garlic cloves

½ teaspoon ground cumin

½ teaspoon dried oregano

1 tablespoon salt

1. Combine the diced pineapple, tomatoes, chopped onion, orange juice, all the chiles, and the garlic, cumin, oregano, and salt in a blender. Blend until smooth.

2. Arrange the pork in a large, nonreactive dish or casserole. Pour the pineapple mixture over the meat. Cover and marinate in the refrigerator for 12 hours.

3. Thirty minutes before cooking, prepare a direct-heat, asado-style fire in your grill to medium heat (see page 27). Be sure the grill is clean so that the meat does not stick.

4. Remove the meat from the refrigerator and grill the pork, the pineapple slices, and the sliced onion until the meat is browned on the outside and firm (the color is hard to judge because of the marinade), the pineapple is marked with char lines but not so cooked that it folds over on itself when you flip it, and the onion has grill marks and is beginning to be translucent, 12 to 15 minutes, turning the meat, pineapple, and onion every few minutes.

1 (5-pound) pork shoulder, cut into steak-size (5-by-3-inch) pieces, ¾-inch thick

40 mini (3-inch) fresh corn tortillas

Chopped fresh cilantro, lemon wedges, sliced jalapeño pepper, and salsa of your choice for serving

5. Chop the pork, onion, and pineapple together, all at once (preferably with a cleaver) to fuse the flavors.

6. Serve the meat mixture in doubled-up, warmed, mini tortillas garnished with chopped cilantro, lemon wedges, jalapeño slices, and salsa.

TACOS DE BIRRIA (GOAT)

MAKES 18 TO 20 MINI TACOS, OR 8 TO 10 SERVINGS   PREP TIME: 10 TO 15 MINUTES, PLUS OVERNIGHT

MARINATING   COOK TIME: 4½ HOURS

Goat meat gives this street taco a unique flavor profile. It is leaner than most meats, including lamb and pork, yet it has a full, slightly gamey taste. This dish is most often found in Jalisco, in northwestern Mexico, where it's frequently served as a soup. Jalisco's capital city, Guadalajara, has restaurants that specialize exclusively in *birria*, and in neighboring states of Mexico you'll find different variations on the same theme. The dish is prepared the same whether you enjoy it as a soup or taco, and it's served at everything from baptisms to weddings and on holidays.

1 tablespoon salt

2 teaspoons ground cumin

1 teaspoon minced fresh oregano

1 teaspoon freshly ground black pepper

5 cloves

½ teaspoon ground cinnamon

1 (10-pound) chivas leg (goat leg)

1 tablespoon manteca (lard) or vegetable oil

6 tomatoes, quartered

1 large white onion

10 guajillo chiles, seeds removed

3 ancho chiles, seeds removed

6 pequin chiles

4 arbol chiles

6 garlic cloves

1 tablespoon ground ginger

5 bay leaves

1. Mix together the salt, cumin, oregano, ½ teaspoon of the black pepper, and the cloves and cinnamon in a small bowl.

2. Rub the meat all over with the spice mixture and marinate in the refrigerator, covered, overnight.

3. Fill a large pot fitted with a steamer one-quarter full (or about 2 inches deep) with water. Bring the water to a boil and add the goat. Steam until the meat is tender, about 2 hours.

4. Remove the meat and reserve the broth for later use.

5. Melt the manteca in a large skillet over medium heat. Add the tomatoes, onion, all the chiles, the garlic, ginger, bay leaves, and epazote, and the remaining ½ teaspoon of black pepper and cook until the onion is soft, 12 to 15 minutes.

6. Transfer the vegetables from the skillet to a blender. Add 2 cups of the reserved goat broth. Blend until smooth to create a sauce, then use a strainer to ensure the sauce is liquid with no chunks.

7. Add the sauce to the original large pot along with the goat meat and cook until the meat pulls easily from the bone leaving the bone clean, about 2 more hours.

1 teaspoon ground epazote

40 mini (3-inch) corn tortillas

Chopped onion, fresh cilantro,
and lime, for garnish

8. Remove the goat meat from the bone, reserving the sauce, and shred the meat, using two forks.

9. Serve the goat meat on doubled-up mini tortillas. Drizzle the sauce over the meat and garnish with chopped onion, cilantro, and lime. The sauce is often served in a small bowl to accompany the tacos, as a goat soup called consomé in Spanish.

TACOS CAMPECHANOS (BEEF WITH CHORIZO AND CHICHARRONES)

MAKES   18 TO 20 MINI TACOS, OR 8 TO 10 SERVINGS   PREP TIME: 5 TO 10 MINUTES, PLUS 1 TO 2 HOURS TO MARINATE   COOK TIME: 15 TO 20 MINUTES

On a trip to Mexico City, I befriended my taxi driver. In true *chilango* (Mexico City native) style, he showed me a taco I had no idea existed. I quickly recognized that this guy knew what he was doing, so, over the next few days, he guided me to obscure local taco shops to try what he thought were the best tacos in town. It was on this trip that I first discovered the *bistec* taco as shared here.

The combination of the deep spices from the chorizo with the texture of the crushed chicharrones gives these tacos an explosion of flavors. I first tried them at a place called El Carnal, whose name translates to "brother" or "very close male friend." The people at that type of taqueria are in fact a band of brothers, in a sense, as you will find construction workers, taxi drivers, or businessmen, all from different walks of life, coming together over tacos.

3 tablespoons water

1 tablespoon olive oil

2 teaspoons ancho chile powder

1 teaspoon salt

1 teaspoon garlic powder

½ teaspoon dried Mexican oregano

½ teaspoon freshly ground black pepper

3 pounds ¼-inch-thick, round steaks

1 large white onion, sliced into 1-inch rounds

3 pounds Spanish-style (chorizo) sausage

40 mini (3-inch) corn tortillas

3 to 4 ounces fried chicharrones, crushed

Chopped onion, fresh cilantro, and lime wedges for serving

1. Mix the water with the oil, ancho chile powder, salt, garlic powder, oregano, and black pepper in a large bowl to form a paste. Add the steak to the bowl and coat it with the spices. Marinate in the refrigerator, covered, for 1 to 2 hours.

2. Two hours before you'd like to begin cooking, prepare a grill asado style (see page 27).

3. Cook the onion slices on the grill over direct heat, turning often, until char marks appear and they're translucent, about 7 minutes total. Meanwhile, grill the beef until browned, 3 to 4 minutes each side, turning as needed.

4. Remove the meat and onion from the grill. Cut into thin strips.

5. Remove the chorizo from its casing. Cook the chorizo in a skillet until cooked through and deep red, not pink, about 7 minutes. Add the beef strips and onion and cook, stirring, to distribute the flavor throughout, 1 to 2 minutes.

6. Put the meat in doubled-up tortillas, then top the tacos with crushed chicharrones for added texture. Serve garnished with chopped onion, cilantro, and lime wedges.

TACOS DE BUCHE (PORK STOMACH)

MAKES **18 TO 20 TACOS, OR 8 TO 10 SERVINGS**   PREP TIME: **15 TO 20 MINUTES**
COOK TIME: **3 TO 4 HOURS**

I find one of the greatest pleasures derived from this dish comes from its texture. Some people enjoy it crispy, some enjoy it suave (soft)—and others like a middle ground between crispy and soft *buche*. The name may be intimidating, but done right, I find these to be a great treat—and I like mine with a crisp texture. Dressings and salsas liven up this dish, and customizing the condiments is key to pleasing everybody at the table.

10 pounds buche (pork stomach)

1 yellow onion

4 garlic cloves

2 ancho chiles

2 jalapeño peppers

2 tablespoons salt

1 tablespoon minced fresh oregano

1 tablespoon manteca (lard) or vegetable oil

40 mini (3-inch) corn tortillas

Chopped fresh cilantro, sliced onion, lemon wedges, jalapeño slices, and your choice of salsas for serving

1. Clean the buche by rinsing it well with cold water.

2. Bring a medium pot of water to a boil. Add the buche to the water and keep on a rolling boil until firm, about 5 minutes.

3. Remove the buche from the water and rinse again under cold water, then allow it to cool.

4. Cut the buche into ¼-inch pieces.

5. Combine the buche, onion, garlic, ancho chiles, jalapeños, salt, and oregano in a medium stockpot. Cover completely with water, 2 inches past the top of the meat. Simmer over medium-low heat until tender, 3 to 4 hours, adding more water as necessary during cooking. Remove the meat from the water and discard the water and seasonings.

6. Melt the manteca in a large skillet over medium heat. Fry the buche meat until deeply browned and crispy, 10 to 15 minutes.

7. Serve the buche in doubled-up mini tortillas with chopped cilantro, onion, lemon wedges, jalapeño, and your choice of salsas.

TRIPAS DE RES TACOS (BEEF TRIPE)

MAKES **18 TO 20 MINI TACOS, OR 8 TO 10 SERVINGS**   PREP TIME: **20 TO 30 MINUTES**
COOK TIME: **10 TO 18 MINUTES**

When served here in South Texas, you'll find *tripas de res* are fried more often than grilled. But I choose to grill them to add the level of crispiness that I prefer. Have it your way, from soft to crispy, as tripas are customizable, dependent on their time on the grill.

8 to 10 pounds tripas de res (beef intestine)

2 tablespoons salt

4 lemons

20 mini (3-inch) corn tortillas

Sliced avocado, Tomatillo Salsa (page 179), chopped fresh cilantro, and onion for serving

1. Bring a large stockpot of water to a boil. Add the tripas and 1 tablespoon of the salt and boil until fully pliable, 45 minutes. Remove the meat from the water and set aside.

2. Build a direct, asado-style fire for your grill (see page 27).

3. Put the meat on the grill over medium-high heat, squeeze the lemon juice over the tripas, and season it with the remaining tablespoon of salt. For a soft texture, grill until gray to golden, not charred and speckled brown, turning the meat two or three times every 2 to 3 minutes, for a total of 5 to 7 minutes. For a crisper, crunchier texture, grill until you see charring and a resemblance to cracklings, turning every 2 to 3 minutes, for a total of 12 to 15 minutes.

4. Remove from the grill and slice the tripas into 2-inch pieces.

5. Serve the tripas on doubled-up mini tortillas garnished with sliced avocado, tomatillo salsa, chopped cilantro, and onion.

TAMALES

Tamales are all about collaboration, from the flavor created by the combination of ingredients to the actual assembly line process of crafting each corn husk packet. What started as delegation of duties to tackle the cumbersome task of making tamales has evolved to what is now called a *tamalada*: a tamale-making gathering that represents family, culture, tradition, and togetherness. Whether they are sweet or savory, your imagination is the only limitation to the variety of your tamale fillings.

First, prep the corn husks and the masa. You can make several fillings, and then do the assembly of all of the tamales at once. Serve them on their own or with beans and rice. And they freeze well, too!

SOAKED TAMALE CORN HUSKS

PREP TIME: SOAK TIME 1 HOUR MINIMUM, OVERNIGHT PREFERRED

2¼ pounds corn husks

1. Put the corn husks in a large bowl, then cover them with hot water, until they are completely submerged, for a minimum of 1 hour, preferably overnight. This step ensures that they are pliable and will not burn during cooking.

2. Remove the husks from the water and pat dry with paper towels. Put them in a covered dish or plastic bag to ensure that they do not dry out.

TAMALE MASA

MAKES **MASA FOR 90 TAMALES**

PREP TIME: **15 MINUTES**

COOK TIME: **5 MINUTES**

4 cups manteca (lard) for frying (vegetable oil cannot substitute)

2 garlic cloves

1 (5-pound) bag masa harina

2 tablespoons baking powder

1 tablespoon salt

8 cups pork broth

1. Melt the manteca in a large skillet over medium-low heat until it reaches a low simmer. Add the garlic and infuse the manteca with the garlic flavor, being sure not to let the garlic brown. Remove the pan from the heat after 5 minutes. Remove garlic cloves.

2. Stir the masa, baking powder, and salt together in a large mixing bowl. Knead the pork broth into the masa until it is completely absorbed.

3. While the garlic-infused manteca is still very hot, knead it into the masa, using your hands (yes, it is hot and, yes, it will hurt a bit) until the masa no longer sticks to your palms. It is important that the masa is not sticky. If it is sticky, add more manteca. Be sure not to add more water, as it will only make it too packed and solid. Set aside until the tamales are ready to fill.

TAMALES VERDES (CHICKEN WITH GREEN SAUCE)

MAKES **30 TAMALES**   PREP TIME: **30 MINUTES**   COOK TIME: **2½ TO 3 HOURS**

This spicy, tangy, and light chicken filling is a delight for those who like a traditional Mexican tamale with a kick.

1 (3- to 4-pound) whole chicken (giblets removed)

¼ yellow onion

2 tablespoons salt

4 garlic cloves

1 pound tomatillos

2 serrano peppers

½ bunch cilantro

Tamales Masa (page 119)

30 presoaked corn husks (see page 118)

1. Put the whole chicken, onion, 1 tablespoon of the salt, and 2 of the garlic cloves in a large pot. Add water to cover. Bring to a boil over high heat and cook until the chicken begins to separate from the bone, 45 minutes to 1 hour. Remove the chicken, reserving the chicken broth for later use.

2. Allow the chicken to cool, then shred the meat, using two forks. Set the chicken aside.

3. Combine the tomatillos, serrano peppers, cilantro, remaining 2 garlic cloves, remaining tablespoon of salt, and 2 cups of the reserved chicken broth in a blender. Blend on high speed until it becomes a smooth, sauce consistency, not a paste. If it is pasty, add more liquid as needed.

4. Warm the chicken and the broth mixture together in a large saucepan over medium heat. Cook until the sauce thickens, 10 to 15 minutes. Remove the saucepan from the heat and put the chicken and broth in a large bowl to allow to cool.

5. To assemble the tamales, take a soaked corn husk and put about ¼ cup (depending on the size of the husk) of prepared tamale masa in the middle of the widest part of the husk. Use a spoon or spatula to spread the masa, covering the corn husk evenly, leaving a ¼-inch border around the edges.

6. Add 3 to 4 tablespoons of filling mixture to the center of the masa. Roll the sides over, enclosing the filling completely. Fold the tapered end of the corn husk up, in half. If desired, you can

secure it closed by tying a strip of husk around the middle. Repeat until you have used up all the filling.

7. Arrange the tamales, with open ends up, in a large, prepared steamer pot or pot fitted with a steaming basket. Steam until the dough separates from the husk, about 1 hour.

TAMALES ROJOS (PORK WITH RED SAUCE)

MAKES **48 TAMALES**   PREP TIME: **30 MINUTES**   COOK TIME: **4 TO 5 HOURS**

This pork tamale is the one that's the most common in South Texas. The red-tinted masa is a familiar sight from Thanksgiving until Christmas on almost any table, whether you're Latino or not. Around here we like to top pork tamales with chili con carne (see Vaquero Chili con Carne, page 134).

1 whole pig head, or one 3½- to 4-pound bone-in pork shoulder

½ yellow onion

2 tablespoons salt

5 garlic cloves

15 guajillo chiles

1 teaspoon ground cumin

Tamales Masa (page 119)

48 presoaked corn husks (see page 118)

1. Combine the pig head, onion, 1 tablespoon of the salt, and 3 of the garlic cloves in a large pot. Cover with water. Bring to a boil over high heat and cook until the pork begins to separate from the bone, 2½ to 3½ hours. Remove the pork and reserve the broth for later use.

2. Allow the pork to cool, then shred the meat using two forks. Set the meat aside.

3. Put the guajillo chiles in a medium saucepan over medium heat and cover them with water. Cook until completely reconstituted, 10 to 12 minutes. Remove the chiles from the water.

4. Combine the guajillo chilis (with their seeds), cumin, remaining two garlic cloves, remaining tablespoon of salt, and 2 cups of the reserved broth in a blender. Blend on high speed until it becomes a smooth, sauce consistency, not a paste. If it is pasty, add more liquid as needed.

5. Stir together the pork and broth mixture in a large saucepan. Cook over low heat until the pork absorbs the sauce, 10 to 15 minutes. Remove from the heat and transfer to a large bowl. Allow to cool.

6. To assemble the tamales, take a soaked corn husk and put about ¼ cup (depending on the size of the husk) of prepared tamale masa in the middle of the widest part of the husk. Use

a spoon or spatula to spread the masa, covering the corn husk evenly, leaving a ¼-inch border around the edges.

7. Add 3 to 4 tablespoons of filling mixture to the center of the masa. Roll the sides over, enclosing the filling completely. Fold the tapered end of the corn husk up, in half. If desired, you can secure it closed by tying a strip of husk around the middle. Repeat until you have used all of the filling.

8. Arrange the tamales, with open ends up, in a large, prepared steamer pot or pot fitted with a steaming basket. Steam until the dough separates from the husk, about 1 hour.

TAMALES RAJAS DE CHILE Y QUESO FRESCO (CHILE AND CHEESE)

MAKES **24 TAMALES**   PREP TIME: **45 MINUTES TO 1 HOUR**   COOK TIME: **1 HOUR**

The textures and simplicity of these ingredients come together to form a combination that just works—and makes this recipe my favorite of the three.

6 poblano chiles

2 teaspoons manteca (lard)

1 yellow onion, sliced

4 tomatoes, cut into wedges

2 tablespoons salt

2 pounds queso fresco

Tamales Masa (page 119)

24 presoaked corn husks (see page 118)

1. Blacken the poblano chiles by placing them on a hot grill, over an open flame, or under the broiler and rotating them as they blister. Remove them from the heat and wrap them in foil to allow them to steam a bit, which helps loosen the skin. Allow to cool.

2. Peel the skin off the poblanos, then cut them into strips.

3. Heat the manteca in a skillet over medium-high heat and add the onion, tomato, and poblano strips. Sauté until the tomato and onion are fully cooked and softened, 6 to 8 minutes. Remove from the heat and set aside.

4. Add the salt and crumble queso fresco into the tomato mixture, folding the mixture to ensure the queso is evenly distributed.

5. To assemble the tamales, take a soaked corn husk and put about ¼ cup (depending on the size of the husk) of prepared tamale masa in the middle of the widest part of the husk. Use a spoon or spatula to spread the masa, covering the corn husk evenly, leaving a ¼-inch border around the edges.

6. Add 3 to 4 tablespoons of filling mixture to the center of the masa. Roll the sides over, enclosing the filling completely. Fold the tapered end of the corn husk up, in half. If desired, you can secure it closed by tying a strip of husk around the middle. Repeat until you have used all of the filling.

7. Arrange the tamales, with open ends up, in a large, prepared steamer pot or pot fitted with a steaming basket. Steam until the dough separates from the husk, about 1 hour.

SOUPS AND CHILIS

Spicy beef chili is widely known to be a big deal in South Texas, but in fact there are a variety of soups and stews that are an important part of the culture. Some of these recipes are usually reserved for special occasions, such as pozole for holidays, and others are legendary for other reasons—such as menudo for breakfast, as a hangover cure. Regardless of the time of day or event, soups make a satisfying meal, especially when you serve them with a homemade tortilla or a hunk of jalapeño corn bread.

MAMA DAVILA'S FIDEO SECO CON CARNE

SERVES **4 TO 6**   PREP TIME: **5 MINUTES**   COOK TIME: **15 TO 20 MINUTES**

This dish was a hands-down favorite of the Davila kids. In retrospect, Mom probably made this recipe the most frequently because she could feed so many with such little effort or cost. But we loved it because of her creativity with this dish. Mom used to switch it up by adding elbow pasta or *conchitas* (shell pasta) instead of traditional *fideo*, or adding cooked pinto beans or diced potatoes. I've included two versions of this recipe. This version is thick and stewlike or "dry," whereas the Sopa de Fideo Estilo Laredo (page 130) is more like a soup.

1 pound 80/20 ground beef

1½ teaspoons salt

1 teaspoon freshly ground black pepper

½ teaspoon garlic powder

5 ounces vermicelli fideo noodles, broken into 2-inch pieces

1 green onion, thinly sliced

½ cup canned tomato sauce

Fresh flour tortillas for serving

1. Cook the ground beef in a medium saucepan over medium heat, seasoning it with ½ teaspoon of the salt, ½ teaspoon of the pepper, and the garlic powder. Cook, stirring, until browned, 6 to 8 minutes.

2. Add the fideo noodles and cook, stirring frequently as the thin noodles can easily burn, until golden brown, 2 to 3 minutes.

3. Add the green onion and cook, stirring, until the onion is translucent, about 3 minutes.

4. Add the tomato sauce, stir, and cook until well combined, about 1 minute.

5. Add the water and remaining teaspoon of salt and ½ teaspoon of pepper (or to taste). Bring to a bubbling simmer. Cover and allow to thicken, about 10 minutes. This process will allow the fideo to become *seco*, or "dry."

6. Serve with fresh flour tortillas.

CALDO DE RES

MAKES **8 TO 10 SERVINGS**   PREP TIME: **5 TO 10 MINUTES**   COOK TIME: **60 TO 75 MINUTES**

To be honest, *caldo de res* is my go-to hangover soup. Most people prefer a chicken soup, but I favor this one with beef because it is heartier. The gelatinous collagen of the oxtail provides extra depth of flavor. This soup is popular throughout South Texas on the weekends, so perhaps I am not alone. It can be made equally well using chicken in place of beef.

5 pounds beef soup bone or oxtail

2 cups beef broth

6 garlic cloves, crushed

2 tablespoons salt

1 teaspoon ground cumin

1 teaspoon freshly ground black pepper

1 large russet potato, cut into 1-inch disks

3 medium chayotes

3 celery ribs, cut into 2-inch-long pieces

2 medium ripe tomatoes, cut into 1-inch cubes

1½ green bell peppers, sliced

1 medium yellow onion, cut into 1-inch squares

½ head cabbage, cut into 2-inch-wide strips

½ bunch fresh cilantro, chopped

1 lemon, cut into wedges

Arroz Mexicano (page 156; optional)

1. Rinse the soup bones or oxtail thoroughly, then put in a large stockpot. Add the beef broth and fill remainder of the pot with water (2 to 3 quarts, depending on the size of the pot).

2. Add the garlic, salt, cumin, and black pepper and bring to boil over high heat. Cook until the meat is no longer red and is starting to become firm, 10 to 15 minutes.

3. Add the potato and cook for 20 minutes more, then add the chayote, celery, tomatoes, bell pepper, and onion and simmer for another 20 to 25 minutes.

4. Add the cabbage and cilantro and cook until the cabbage is soft and translucent, 5 to 8 minutes.

5. To serve, divide among bowls and squeeze a little lemon over each for an additional flavor burst. Serve alone as a full meal or stir in some of the Arroz Mexicano for extra texture.

SOPA DE FIDEO ESTILO LAREDO

SERVES 6 TO 8   PREP TIME: 5 TO 10 MINUTES   COOK TIME: 25 TO 30 MINUTES

This is a traditional Mexican dish, favored for its taste, ease of preparation, and economical appeal. It's a very popular dish in my family and beyond. This version is the way you will find it prepared and presented in Mexico, using fresh tomatoes and garlic, sautéing them to bring out their own unique flavor profile. As opposed to the Fideo Seco con Carne (page 128), this dish is served with broth, as a soup. Note that when you buy this type of fideo pasta, it comes looking like a ball of yarn.

½ cup manteca (lard) or vegetable oil

4 ounces fideo pasta (Goya makes the nest/ball-like fideo)

3 medium extra-ripe tomatoes (about 1 pound), roughly chopped

½ medium yellow onion, roughly chopped

3 garlic cloves

1 teaspoon freshly ground black pepper

3 cups chicken broth

Queso fresco, crumbled, for serving

Sliced avocado, for serving

1. Heat the oil in a large saucepan over medium heat. Stir in the fideo pasta, breaking it in 2- to 3-inch strands, and cook, stirring gently and continuously to prevent breaking or burning the pasta strands, until golden brown, 2 to 3 minutes. Be very gentle as the pasta can break down into rice-size pieces if you're not careful.

2. Combine the tomatoes, onion, and garlic in a blender and puree until smooth.

3. Drain the oil, leaving only about 2 teaspoons in the saucepan.

4. Add the blended vegetables and the black pepper to the pasta in the saucepan.

5. Raise the temperature under the saucepan to high heat, and continue to cook, stirring the sauce, until the sauce thickens, 4 minutes.

6. Add the chicken broth and bring the mixture to a boil. Lower the heat and simmer until the pasta is completely cooked and soft, 10 to 12 minutes.

7. Serve in bowls, topped with queso fresco and avocado.

CHICKEN TORTILLA SOUP

SERVES 6 TO 8   PREP TIME: 10 TO 15 MINUTES   COOK TIME: 1 HOUR

There are many variations of this popular chicken soup, from very deep red and thick, with a multitude of ingredients in the southwestern style, to the clear and light flavors of this more authentically Mexican version. In my opinion, tortilla soup has been commercialized in unnecessary ways in the Americanized recipes, with flavors being pulled from too many directions. My recipe celebrates simple, fresh flavors coming together in the bowl.

1 (2½- to 3-pound) whole chicken (giblets removed)

1 gallon water

½ yellow onion

4 garlic cloves

1 tablespoon Knorr brand bouillon powder

1 tablespoon salt

1 teaspoon freshly ground black pepper

2 cups canned chopped tomatoes

Juice of 2 fresh limes

2 whole serrano chiles, sliced into very thin circles

8 sprigs cilantro

2 large, ripe avocados, peeled, pitted, and sliced

1 cup finely grated pepper Jack

2 cups fried corn tortilla strips or broken prepared tortilla chips

1. Put the whole, uncut chicken in a large stockpot over high heat, and cover with the water.

2. Add onion, garlic, bouillon, salt, and pepper. Cover with a lid and cook at a low boil until the chicken easily debones, 40 to 45 minutes. Remove the chicken, reserving the broth. Lower the heat to a simmer.

3. Bone the chicken, discarding the skin, bones, and cartilage and reserving the meat. Using two forks, shred the chicken into large chunks—do not shred finely, as the meat will continue to break down after returning to the broth.

4. Add the chicken back to the broth as well as the chopped tomatoes, lime juice, and chiles. Chop half of the cilantro and add to the pot. Simmer until the flavors blend well, about 15 minutes.

5. Serve in bowls topped with avocado, grated cheese, the remaining cilantro, and the tortilla strips.

POZOLE ROJO DE PUERCO (RED PORK POZOLE)

SERVES 10 TO 12   PREP TIME: 5 TO 10 MINUTES   COOK TIME: 1 HOUR

Pozole has ritual significance as a community dish, dating back to the Aztecs. Typically, in Mexico City, Thursday is pozole day, but no matter the occasion, this celebrated dish makes for a great meal. I did not grow up eating pozole, as it wasn't commonly found in South Texas until recently. But I became familiar with it through my Mexican-born employees, who enjoy making it for birthdays and holidays, such as New Year's. Red pozole has a bold, earthy, and savory taste that's a bit addictive, and, unlike *menudo* (see page 136), this dish is all about the different toppings.

POZOLE:

8 pounds espinazo (pork backbone)

½ yellow onion

3½ tablespoons salt

4 garlic cloves

2 (108-ounce, or 6-pound) cans hominy, liquid drained

CHILE SAUCE:

½ cup water

4 ounces ancho chiles

4 ounces cascabel chiles

3 garlic cloves

1 tablespoon salt

1 teaspoon ground cumin

Your choice of thinly sliced jalapeño, radish, and avocado; fried tortilla strips; shredded cabbage; and chicharonnes for serving

1. Place pork in large stockpot over high heat and add water to cover. Add the remaining pozole ingredients, except for the hominy. Bring the mixture to medium boil and cook until the pork is gray, no longer pink, 20 to 25 minutes.

2. Stir in the hominy and cook until the hominy begins to soften, an additional 10 to 15 minutes.

3. Meanwhile, make the sauce: Combine all the sauce ingredients in a blender. Blend until completely smooth, 2 to 3 minutes.

4. Add the chile sauce to the pork and continue to cook until the pork is fork-tender, 10 to 15 more minutes. Remove the onion.

5. Add your own unique touch to this classic Mexican dish by serving it with toppings of your choice, such as jalapeño, radish, and avocado slices; tortilla strips; shredded cabbage; and chicharonnes.

VAQUERO CHILI CON CARNE

SERVES 8 TO 10   **PREP TIME: 10 MINUTES**   **COOK TIME: 1½ TO 2 HOURS**

One of the most iconic vaquero dishes is chili con carne, and it's such a part of the fabric of the culture that it's considered the national dish of Texas. Chili con carne was likely developed on the range, as a heavy, high-yield, protein-filled dish made by cooking lesser cuts of meat over a long period of time. But the origin of its popularity is often traced to downtown San Antonio, around the plaza at the Alamo, where the chili queens used to stir their pots and sell their goods—they even sold their chilis at the Columbian Exposition in Chicago in 1893.

I use different adaptations of this recipe for my enchilada fillings, and it can also be used on hot dogs or fries. My grandmother Davila would make chili when it was cold outside, and one day I convinced her to let me peer over her shoulder as she did her work. Our chili con carne is a little spicy, but as my grandmother proclaimed, if you're going to make chili in Texas, it'd better be spicy.

5 pounds coarsely ground chuck

1 cup chili powder

3 bay leaves

2¼ teaspoons minced garlic

2¼ teaspoons salt

2¼ teaspoons freshly ground
   black pepper

1½ teaspoons onion powder

1½ teaspoons ground cumin

1 teaspoon cayenne pepper

¾ teaspoon dried oregano

1 cup chopped canned tomatoes

½ cup canned tomato sauce

¼ cup beef broth

1. Put the meat in a large stockpot or, preferably, a large Dutch oven. Fill with water until it just covers meat, then bring to a simmer. Simmer over medium heat until the meat is gray, not pink, and firm, 25 to 30 minutes. Pouring over a colander, drain the water from the stockpot. (This step also removes excess fat.)

2. Season the meat in the stockpot with the chili powder, bay leaves, garlic, salt, black pepper, onion powder, cumin, cayenne, and oregano.

3. Stir in the canned tomatoes, tomato sauce, and beef broth. Add water to cover to a depth of 2 inches above the meat. Stir all the ingredients.

4. Cook, uncovered, over medium heat, at a simmer, not a boil, until the beef is tender, 45 minutes to an hour. Stir in the pinto beans, if using.

2 cups cooked pinto beans
(optional)

Chopped onion and grated
Cheddar for serving

South Texas Jalapeño Cheese
Corn Bread (page 169;
optional) for serving

5. Top with chopped onion and grated Cheddar, and serve
accompanied with corn bread, if desired.

MENUDO DE PUERCO

SERVES 10   PREP TIME: **20 TO 30 MINUTES, PLUS 2 HOURS OF SOAK TIME**   COOK TIME: **4 HOURS**

Menudo is a traditional Mexican soup often served after big celebrations. White menudo is served in the Mexican state of Sinaloa, but hominy only finds its way into this dish when it comes to South Texas, where it's sort of a combination of menudo and pozole. A question I still haven't been able to answer is: When and why did Texans start adding hominy to this dish? Here I pay homage to the original Mexican recipe, and don't use any hominy. If you haven't cooked with tripe (also called hog maw) before, it's the muscular portion of the stomach, and not at all fatty if properly cleaned. You can fry it, stew it, or broil it—and even make tacos out of it.

MENUDO:

4 pounds honeycomb tripe

2 gallons water

1½ pounds pig's feet

2 garlic cloves

¼ yellow onion

1½ teaspoons salt

SAUCE:

1 chile de arbol, stemmed and seeded

3 guajillo chiles, stemmed and seeded

1½ teaspoons dried oregano

1 garlic clove

1 bay leaf

1. Rinse the honeycomb tripe and cut it into 1-inch squares.

2. Soak the tripe in water for 2 hours in the refrigerator, changing the water after an hour.

3. Combine the 2 gallons of fresh water with the pig's feet, garlic, onion, and salt in a large stockpot over high heat. Bring to a boil then reduce to medium-low heat. Simmer, uncovered, until the tripe begins to soften, 1 hour.

4. Toast the chiles on a dry skillet over medium heat until fragrant, about 30 seconds. Pour enough water over the chiles to cover, and allow to simmer over low heat, soaking the chiles.

5. Combine the remaining sauce ingredients and the chiles in a blender. Add 2 cups of the broth from the soup to the blender and puree—be careful, as it will be hot.

6. After the tripe has been cooking for 1 hour, add the sauce to the stockpot and continue to cook until the tripe is tender but not falling apart, an additional 2½ to 3 hours.

½ teaspoon salt

½ teaspoon freshly ground black
    pepper

Diced onion, chopped fresh
    cilantro, lemon wedges, and
    thinly sliced jalapeños for
    serving

7. Serve in bowls and top with diced onion, chopped cilantro, lemon wedges, and thinly sliced jalapeños.

POZOLE VERDE DE POLLO (GREEN CHICKEN POZOLE)

SERVES 10 TO 12   PREP TIME: 5 TO 10 MINUTES   COOK TIME: 1 HOUR

Just like red, green pozole is often reserved for special occasions. Although it's a very simple dish, the condiments add depth and texture. This variation originates from the state of Guerrero in Mexico. It's most often made with chicken but can also be made with pork—or make it with pork *and* chicken. The chicken adds a nice firm texture, while the pork lends juiciness because of its fat content. It's fun to create your own bowl with the colorful, zesty combinations of toppings, which add a lot of flair to your table.

SOUP:

2 (3- to 3½-pound) chickens, each cut into 8 pieces

2 (108-ounce, or 6-pound) cans hominy

1 whole garlic head

½ yellow onion

SAUCE:

2 poblano peppers

½ pound tomatillos

2 serrano peppers

½ cup toasted pumpkin seeds (optional; see note)

½ bunch cilantro

2 garlic cloves

3 teaspoons salt

Your choice of thinly sliced jalapeño, radish, and avocado; tortilla strips; shredded cabbage; and chicharonnes, for serving

1. Combine the soup ingredients in a large stockpot over high heat. Cover with water and bring to a boil. Once boiling, turn the heat down to a simmer and cook until the chicken starts to separate from the bone, 45 minutes.

2. Meanwhile, make the sauce: Roast the poblano peppers, rotating them under the broiler or over an open flame, asado style, until the skin is blackened, 5 to 7 minutes. Put them in a plastic bag and allow to sweat for 5 to 7 minutes.

3. While the peppers are in the bag, prepare the tomatillos: Put the tomatillos in a saucepan over high heat and cover them with water. Bring to a boil and boil until the skin begins to split open, 7 to 8 minutes.

4. As the tomatillos are boiling, remove the poblano peppers from the plastic bag. Use a paper towel or a kitchen towel to rub the skin off the pepper and peel it from the flesh. Alternatively, peel the skin off the peppers by using your hands to rub it off under cold running water, then dry them. Remove the stems.

5. Combine the poblanos, cooked tomatillos, and the remaining sauce ingredients in a blender. Blend until pureed, adding up to a cup of water, as needed, to ensure that the sauce blends smoothly.

NOTE: Toast the pumpkin seeds in a dry pan over medium-high heat until they're popping and a nutty aroma is released, 3 to 4 minutes. They add a unique smoky, nutty flavor to the dish.

6. Add the sauce to the stockpot and cook until it thickens, an additional 15 minutes. Remove the onion and garlic.

7. Add your own unique touch to this classic Mexican dish by serving it with toppings of your choice, such as jalapeño, radish, and avocado slices; tortilla strips; shredded cabbage; and chicharonnes.

ON THE SIDE

VEGETABLES AND SIDES

This chapter showcases a mix of influences, from South Texas, Mexico, and beyond, with a multitude of vibrant colors, textures, and zesty flavor combinations. It's punctuated with heirloom recipes that were passed down to me, such as Grandma's Papas and Arroz Mexicano, which hold some of my dearest childhood memories. I like to keep traditional recipes, such as Grilled Nopales and Camotes over Coals, simple and authentic, using fresh ingredients and basic (sometimes primal) techniques.

BUTTERNUT SQUASH WITH CHILE AND LIME

SERVES 4 TO 6   **PREP TIME: 5 MINUTES**   **COOK TIME: 75 TO 90 MINUTES**

The spice and tang of the chile combined with the sweetness of the squash add to the versatility of this dish. Serve it serve hot or cold, as a side or appetizer. It makes a perfect snack, pulled out of the fridge as a cool reward during the hot summer months of South Texas.

1 large (about 2-pound) butternut
    squash

4 limes

2 tablespoons Tajín Clásico
    Seasoning (chile-lime salt)

1. Preheat the oven to 325°F.

2. Wrap the butternut squash in foil and put it in the oven, directly on the grate. Cook until the skin begins to loosen, 15 to 20 minutes.

3. Remove the squash from the oven, unwrap it, and cut it in half lengthwise. Using a spoon, remove the seeds and strands and discard them.

4. Peel the skin completely off the squash.

5. Squeeze the limes over the squash and rub the chili-lime salt over all sides.

6. Wrap the squash in foil again and return it to the oven. Cook until softened, about 75 minutes. Remove the squash from the oven and allow it to cool.

7. Cut the squash into 2-inch cubes. Serve warm or chilled as a side or appetizer.

ELOTE CON CREMA (CREAMED CORN)

SERVES **6 TO 8**   PREP TIME: **5 MINUTES**   COOK TIME: **30 TO 45 MINUTES**

Elote con crema is one of the easiest dishes in this book, but it's packed with the biggest reward—people love it. In Zócalo Square in Mexico City, men and women peddle it in their carts, boisterous salesmen. I can hear them now, *"Elote fresco, elote calientito, elote sabroso!"* The hot cup and aroma is a soothing and rich treat that pairs well with other street foods (see pages 109–124), and it's simple and cheap. Here in Seguin, corn continues to be an important and vital part of our economy and culture, as local farmers depend on it, planting vast crops. Serve this as a side with any style of barbecue, or in a cup as a snack or appetizer.

4 tablespoons salted butter

1¼ pounds frozen corn (not canned)

¾ pound whole-milk cream cheese

¼ cup sugar

2 teaspoons salt

½ teaspoon freshly ground black pepper

½ cup grated Parmesan

Tajín Clásico Seasoning (chile-lime salt)

1. Melt the butter in a skillet over low heat and add the frozen corn. Let the corn cook until soft, 5 to 8 minutes.

2. Add the cream cheese, sugar, salt, and pepper and mix together. Cover and cook over low heat, stirring frequently to prevent burning, until the cream cheese completely melts and becomes a saucelike consistency.

3. Stir in the Parmesan.

4. Serve with the chile-lime salt liberally sprinkled over the top.

CALABACITAS CON FRIJOLES NEGROS (ZUCCHINI WITH BLACK BEANS)

SERVES **4 TO 6**   PREP TIME: **10 MINUTES, PLUS 12 HOURS TO SOAK BEANS**   COOK TIME: **1½ HOURS**

Bright colors and different textures give this dish flair—we eat first with our eyes, after all. It can be served hot, as a side dish, or cold, like a salad, and it pairs well with pork, beef, fish, or chicken.

1 pound dried black beans, rinsed thoroughly

4 cups water

1 large white onion, diced

1 green bell pepper, diced

3 tablespoons olive oil

3 garlic cloves, finely chopped

1 bay leaf

2 cups diced zucchini (about 1 large)

2 cups diced yellow summer squash (about 1 large)

1 teaspoon ground cumin

1 teaspoon dried oregano

2 teaspoons salt

1 teaspoon freshly ground black pepper

1. Sort and clean the beans, removing any dirt, rocks, or fragments.

2. Soak the beans in water for 10 to 12 hours.

3. Combine the beans with 4 cups of fresh water, half of the diced onion, all of the bell pepper, 2 tablespoons of the oil, and the garlic and bay leaf in a large stockpot over high heat. Bring to a boil, then lower the heat to medium and simmer until the beans are soft, about 1 hour, checking regularly and skimming away any foam that floats to the surface.

4. Heat the remaining tablespoon of olive oil in a large skillet over medium heat. Stir in the zucchini, summer squash, the remaining diced onion, and the cumin, oregano, salt, and black pepper. Cook until the vegetables begin to soften, about 2 minutes.

5. Lower the heat to a simmer and cook, covered, stirring frequently, until slightly thickened and the zucchini has softened, 8 to 10 minutes.

6. Remove the bay leaf, stir the vegetables into the beans, and serve.

FRIJOLES BORRACHOS (DRUNKEN BEANS)

SERVES **10 TO 12**   PREP TIME: **8 TO 10 MINUTES, PLUS 12 HOURS TO SOAK BEANS (OPTIONAL)**

COOK TIME: **1 HOUR 15 MINUTES**

I like to say that "drunken" refers to the plethora of meats in this otherwise simple bean dish—the first people to make it must have been a little tipsy to add so many things to a simple pot of beans! It's almost like a soup, with tomatoes and onion in addition to three meats, and I like to serve it in the cooler months as the chiles warm your insides up. But my primary memories of making this side dish involve a lot of machismo . . . and beer. I'd be tasked with cleaning and sorting the beans, then all the men in the family would cook this, standing over the pot while grilling the rest of the dinner, and drinking. Serve it as they did, alongside beef fajitas or your favorite steak dish.

1 pound dried pinto beans, rinsed

3 quarts water

¾ teaspoon salt

3 ancho peppers

3 chipotle peppers in adobo sauce (whole)

¼ pound hot dogs, cut into 1-inch slices

¼ pound sliced deli ham, cut into 1-inch-thick strips

½ pound bacon, cooked and chopped, with drippings

2 medium tomatoes, cut into 1½-inch cubes

½ large yellow onion, cut into 1½-inch cubes

½ cup chopped fresh cilantro

½ cup dark Mexican beer

1. Sort and clean the beans, removing any dirt, rocks, or fragments.

2. Soak the beans in water for 12 hours or overnight (optional). The soaking starts the hydration process and loosens the starch, allowing the beans to cook faster.

3. Drain the beans and put them in a large stockpot. Add 3 quarts of fresh water. Cover and turn the heat to high.

4. Once the water begins to boil, add the salt. Cook over high heat, at a rolling boil, until the beans are soft, about 1 hour.

5. Toast the ancho peppers over a flame or under the broiler for 3 or 4 seconds.

6. Stir the whole chipotle and ancho peppers into the beans. Cook until the ancho peppers are reconstituted, 8 to 10 minutes.

7. Add the hot dogs, ham, bacon, tomatoes, onion, cilantro, and beer. Cook until the tomatoes are stewed, another 8 to 10 minutes, and serve.

FRIJOLES REFRITOS (REFRIED BEANS)

SERVES **8 TO 10**   PREP TIME: **20 TO 30 MINUTES, PLUS 12 HOURS TO SOAK BEANS (OPTIONAL)**

COOK TIME: **1 HOUR 15 MINUTES**

While I was growing up, my favorite refried beans were made by my Grandma Gracie DeLaGarza. I loved how they had a thinner consistency, unlike the thick paste that most refried beans were at the time. I didn't understand the reason behind that technique then, but it's clear to me now that she had to stretch the recipe—because she had to feed 12 kids. Beans of all types seem to be just as prevalent as chile peppers in Mexican cuisine, and there's good reason for that: They're an important source of protein.

My version adds bacon drippings—these are definitely a Texan, meaty BBQ-guy-comin'-at-you style of beans. The drippings add moisture and a smoky saltiness that really complements the pintos. Serve them topped with cheese, in a tortilla, or alongside enchiladas.

2 pounds dried pinto beans, rinsed

1½ gallons water

1 tablespoon salt

3 garlic cloves

½ yellow onion, cut into 2 quarters

1 cup manteca (lard) or vegetable oil

½ cup bacon drippings

1. Sort and clean the dried beans, removing any dirt, rocks, or fragments.

2. Soak the beans in water for 12 hours or overnight (optional). The soaking starts the hydration process and loosens the starch, allowing the beans to cook faster.

3. Drain the beans and put them in a large stockpot. Add 1½ gallons of fresh water. Cover and turn the heat to high.

4. Once the water begins to boil, add the salt, garlic, and ¼ onion. Cook over high heat at a rolling boil until the beans are soft, about 1 hour.

5. Drain the water from the beans.

6. Melt the manteca in a skillet over high heat and add the remaining ¼ onion, sliced. Cook, stirring, until the onion is translucent but not brown, about 4 minutes.

7. Stir in the drained beans and then smash them with a potato masher. As you mash, work in the bacon drippings. Continue to mash until the mixture begins to look like a puree.

8. Simmer over low heat so that beans do not stick, and continue to mash them until they are very smooth, another 5 to 8 minutes.

9. Serve immediately.

GRILLED NOPALES, ONIONS, AND TOMATOES

SERVES **6 TO 8**   PREP TIME: **5 TO 10 MINUTES**   COOK TIME: **15 MINUTES**

This dish screams "Mexican backyard barbecue." The grilled tomatoes, onions, and nopales are a natural marriage of flavors and textures. Scoring the nopale paddles before you grill allows them to secrete the juices. Avoid overgrilling them; the ideal texture is a bit al dente. I find that this dish goes best with flavorful pork ribs or any pork dish.

8 to 10 fresh nopal paddles

¼ cup olive oil

1 tablespoon salt

1½ teaspoons freshly ground black pepper

1½ teaspoons garlic powder

½ teaspoon ground cumin

1 medium yellow onion, cut into ½-inch slices

1½ pounds tomatoes, cut into 1½-inch-thick slices

1. Prepare the grill for direct asado style (see page 27).

2. Put the nopal paddles in a large, glass baking dish and brush them thoroughly with olive oil. Season with the salt, pepper, garlic powder, and cumin on all sides.

3. Put the onion, tomatoes, and nopales on the grill. Grill over medium heat, turning them until they're soft with grill marks but not charred, 12 to 14 minutes. Remove from the grill.

4. Cut the ingredients into bite-size pieces and serve mixed together in a bowl.

NOPALES SALAD

SERVES 6 TO 8   PREP TIME: 15 MINUTES   COOK TIME: 25 MINUTES

Nopales are deeply associated with Mexican heritage and culture—note their symbolic appearance on the national flag—and they hold an equally important role in the historic gastronomy of the region. In the 15th century, explorers prized them for their alleged ability to prevent scurvy and stave off hunger. And in the harsh climate of northern Mexico and South Texas, you can still easily find these thorny paddles growing wild. Readily adopted into the local cuisine for their health properties, their sometimes unappetizing, slippery texture was dealt with by slicing or scoring the skin before cooking. I find a hot grill also does wonders, as showcased in this salad, which works well as a side dish or as a filling for tacos.

8 to 10 fresh nopal paddles

1 corn cob

¼ cup olive oil, 1 teaspoon reserved for drizzling

Salt and freshly ground black pepper

2 large tomatoes, seeded and chopped

4 pickled jalapeño peppers, chopped, including 1½ tablespoons of their brining liquid

Juice of 1 lime

2 tablespoons chopped fresh cilantro

½ teaspoon dried oregano

Leaf lettuce for serving

1 large avocado, peeled, pitted, and sliced

¼ cup crumbled queso fresco

1. Two hours before you want to start cooking, preheat the grill for direct, asado-style, high heat (see page 27).

2. Brush the nopal paddles and corn cob with the olive oil and season them with salt and pepper.

3. Grill the nopales and corn over hot coals until slightly charred, about 5 minutes on each side.

4. Slice the nopales into 1-inch strips and cut the corn kernels off the cob.

5. Combine the nopales, corn, tomatoes, jalapeños and brine, lime juice, 1 teaspoon of salt, ½ teaspoon of black pepper, and the cilantro and oregano in a large bowl. Add a light drizzle, about 1 teaspoon, of olive oil. Set aside for 45 minutes to allow the ingredients to marinate.

6. Serve atop a bed of lettuce, garnished with sliced avocado and queso fresco just before serving.

GRANDPA DAVILA'S POTATO SALAD

SERVES **12 TO 15**   PREP TIME: **30 MINUTES**   COOK TIME: **30 TO 45 MINUTES**

In the early 1950s, at the beginning of the Davila BBQ legacy, my uncle Adolph had a gasoline and goods store with a barbecue restaurant inside. The establishment was called Magnolia Food Market as it was on Magnolia Street in Luling, Texas. My grandfather and his brother served this potato salad at their restaurant, but they most likely formulated this recipe long before then. In their prior life, before being involved in a business, they were cooks and always cooking with their families. It's not served hot so you wouldn't call it quite German, but the pickle and the touch of mustard bring some tanginess to the Davila style of potato salad.

3 pounds russet potatoes, peeled

1 large egg

2 celery ribs, finely chopped

¼ green bell pepper, diced

¼ medium yellow onion, diced

¼ cup sweet relish

¼ cup diced sweet pepper

¼ cup sugar

½ teaspoon salt

½ teaspoon freshly ground black pepper

½ cup mayonnaise

1 teaspoon prepared yellow mustard

1. Bring the potatoes to a boil in a large pot of water and boil until soft, 25 to 30 minutes.

2. Drain the potatoes, mash them a bit (you want them to remain slightly lumpy), and set them aside to cool.

3. Meanwhile, bring a small saucepan of water to a boil and boil the egg for 15 minutes. Allow the egg to cool, then peel and finely chop it.

4. Stir together the egg, celery, bell pepper, onion, sweet relish, and sweet pepper in a medium bowl.

5. Stir the sugar, salt, and pepper into the cooled, mashed potatoes.

6. Stir the vegetable mixture, mayonnaise, and mustard into the potatoes. Mix thoroughly and serve.

GRANDMA'S PAPAS

SERVES **8**   PREP TIME: **10 MINUTES**   COOK TIME: **30 TO 35 MINUTES**

I can still see, smell, and hear the sounds of my grandmother in the kitchen preparing this dish with no measurements and no timer. I'd anxiously wait to have this comforting and savory marriage of potato, tomato, and onion with a hint of garlic. This was my favorite dish by Grandma and now I share it with you. Serve these potatoes alongside beans, corn, or squash, paired with chicken, beef, or pork.

½ cup manteca (lard) or vegetable oil

2 large russet potatoes (1 pound), peeled and cut into ½-inch-thick disks, then cut in half again to make half-moon shapes

1 tablespoon salt

1 teaspoon freshly ground black pepper

½ yellow onion, sliced into ½-inch-thick strips

4 large garlic cloves, minced

2 cups chopped canned tomatoes

1 teaspoon chicken bouillon powder

2 cups warm water

1. Melt the manteca in a large skillet over medium heat, allowing it to heat for 2 to 3 minutes.

2. Add the potatoes, salt, and pepper, and cook, stirring frequently so that they don't stick, until browned, 7 to 9 minutes. This browning step is to remove some moisture so that the potatoes don't become soggy and fall apart later on in the recipe.

3. Add the onion slices and cook, gently stirring, until they begin to soften, 2 to 3 minutes.

4. Add the garlic and continue to cook, stirring gently so that the potatoes do not break apart, until the garlic is fragrant, 1 to 2 minutes.

5. Add the chopped tomatoes and stir until they're softened and warmed through, 2 to 3 minutes.

6. Stir the bouillon powder into the warm water, mixing until the bouillon dissolves.

7. Stir the broth into the skillet and simmer until the liquid begins to thicken, forming a sauce consistency, and the potatoes are cooked through but not falling apart, 8 to 10 minutes. Serve.

CAMOTES (SWEET POTATOES) OVER COALS

MAKES **2 TO 4 SERVINGS**   PREP TIME: **5 MINUTES**   COOK TIME: **30 MINUTES**

I can still hear the steam whistle, which sounds like a large teakettle, from the carts full of camotes in Mexico City. These sweet potatoes are often eaten as a hearty snack or a lunchtime meal. From the streets of Mexico to my restaurant . . . I adopted this method out of a necessity for speed while on the show *BBQ Blitz*. I thought we would have 45 minutes to cook, so I would have plenty of time to bake the sweet potatoes. When we were only given 30, I quickly wrapped them in foil and threw them on the fire, as I had seen my friend Alex Perez do so many times. As a treat, flavor the cooked sweet potatoes with a drizzle of piloncillo (or brown sugar), butter, and cinnamon.

2 sweet potatoes

½ teaspoon salt

1. Two hours before you'd like to start cooking, prepare grill asado style (see page 27).

2. Individually place each potato on a 12-by-24-inch piece of foil.

3. Sprinkle a pinch of salt on each potato, then wrap them in the foil.

4. Place the potato packets directly on the embers of the fire. Cook until soft but not crumbling, about 30 minutes total (the cook time may vary based on the heat of the fire), turning once or twice while cooking. Serve whole or sliced in half.

ARROZ MEXICANO (MEXICAN RICE)

SERVES **8 TO 10**   PREP TIME: **5 TO 10 MINUTES**   COOK TIME: **25 TO 30 MINUTES**

This recipe has a special place in my heart. More than 25 years ago, as a young cook, I learned how to make this dish from my Aunt Esther . . . who likely learned it from my Grandma DeLaGarza on my mom's side. It's one of the few culinary contributions from the DeLaGarzas, yet they still greatly influenced my cooking. That side of my family is more musically inclined, from Grammy-winning artists (David DeLaGarza from La Mafia) to members of the next generation who are forming their own identity as musicians today (notably my niece Julissa, who sang at the Vatican for the pope at Mass on New Year's). I attribute my creativity in the kitchen to these influences.

Often called Spanish rice, this dish has many variations, yet remains a true staple of Latin cuisine. Serve it alone or alongside any style of beans. I like it best paired with Davila's mesquite-smoked Caribbean-Style Whole Red Snapper (page 104).

½ cup manteca (lard) or vegetable oil

2 cups long-grain white rice

½ large green bell pepper, chopped into 1-inch pieces

¼ large yellow onion

¾ teaspoon salt

¾ teaspoon garlic powder

1 teaspoon freshly ground black pepper

1 teaspoon ground cumin

¼ cup chopped tomato

½ cup tomato sauce

4 cups water

1. Melt the manteca in a medium skillet over medium heat.

2. Stir in the rice and cook, stirring constantly, until it turns a pale, golden color, 4 to 5 minutes.

3. Add the bell pepper and onion and cook, stirring, until they start to soften, 3 minutes.

4. Add the salt, garlic powder, black pepper, and cumin and cook, stirring, for 1 minute, or until the cumin and garlic are fragrant. Do not to cook for too long or the spices will burn.

5. Stir in the chopped tomato, tomato sauce, and water.

6. Before the liquid begins to boil, stir all the ingredients to ensure they are thoroughly mixed. Once the water reaches the boiling point, do not stir, as it can cause the rice to be mushy. Cover tightly with a lid and lower the heat to a low simmer. Cook at a low simmer until the liquid is completely absorbed, 12 to 15 minutes. Serve.

ARROZ VERDE (GREEN TOMATILLO RICE)

SERVES **8 TO 10**   PREP TIME: **5 TO 10 MINUTES**   COOK TIME: **25 TO 30 MINUTES**

I first enjoyed this dish in Chachala in Hidalgo, Mexico. Chachala is a city in deep, central Mexico with a total population of 295. My friend Alex Perez taught me how to make this tangy alternative to Arroz Mexicano (page 156). The rice is very green, with lots of pepper, tomatillos, cilantro, and romaine coloring the grains, but the combination doesn't overpower your taste buds. It's an exceptionally tasty and not spicy flavor that works alone, with pork, fish, or, my favorite way, alongside Tinga de Pollo (page 89).

2 poblano peppers, seeds removed, roughly chopped

4 medium tomatillos

1 bunch cilantro

4 romaine lettuce leaves

3 green onions

½ cup cold water

⅔ cup manteca (lard) or vegetable oil

2 cups long-grain converted rice

½ yellow onion, thinly sliced

4 garlic cloves, minced

4 cups chicken broth

½ teaspoon salt

1 lime

1. Start with the green ingredients: Combine the poblanos, tomatillo, cilantro, lettuce, green onion, and the cold water in a blender. Blend until smooth and set aside.

2. Melt the manteca in a medium skillet over medium heat. Add the rice and cook, stirring constantly, until it turns a pale, golden color, 4 to 6 minutes.

3. Add the onion and cook, stirring, for 2 minutes, then add the garlic and stir until the garlic and onion begin to soften, 1 to 2 minutes more.

4. Add the blended green mixture and cook, stirring, until well combined, another 1 to 2 minutes.

5. Add the chicken broth and salt. Before the liquid begins to boil, stir all the ingredients to ensure they are thoroughly mixed. Once the broth reaches the boiling point, do not stir as it can cause the rice to become mushy. Cover tightly with lid and lower the heat to a low simmer. Cook at a low simmer until the liquid is completely absorbed, 8 to 10 minutes. Remove from the heat.

6. When the rice is plated, squeeze the lime over the top just before serving to add an extra burst of flavor.

TORTILLAS AND BREADS

From Cancún, Mexico, to Laredo, Texas, you will find a tortilla accompanying almost every Mexican dish, and a common expression is "If there's not chile or tortillas, it's not a meal." What impresses me most is that the traditional process of making the ubiquitous and all-important corn tortilla started with gathering corn, then cleaning, boiling, and grinding it into a flour and forming the tortillas, all by hand. It was a rigorous physical process that people did on a daily basis just to nourish their families. Out of great need, adults and children gathered together on a communal level to make meals and sides, and tortilla making was (and still remains) an important ritual for family bonding.

For me, bread has always been the ultimate homemade comfort food. There was nothing like the smell of the pan de campo in the oven, filling the house on a cold February morning, or the sound of that rolling pin hitting the board, announcing I was in for a delicious, freshly made flour tortilla. For every meal, or for a small snack with a pat of butter, we always had some form of fresh bread in the kitchen.

PAN DE CAMPO (COUNTRY BREAD)

MAKES 2 (12- TO 14-INCH-DIAMETER, ¾- TO 1-INCH THICK) TORTILLAS   **PREP TIME: 45 MINUTES**

COOK TIME: 20 TO 25 MINUTES

Pan de campo is similar to the flour tortilla, but it's bigger in size and we eat it with different foods. It's delicious on a rainy day with a hearty chili con carne or simply spread with extra butter sprinkled with cinnamon and sugar. It also works well with soup because it's thick and doesn't crumble if you dip it into hot broth.

1½ cups whole milk

3⅓ cups (1 pound) all-purpose flour

2 tablespoons baking powder

1 tablespoon salt

1 cup vegetable shortening

2 tablespoons salted butter or margarine, melted

1. Preheat the oven to 325°F.

2. Gently warm the milk in a small saucepan.

3. Sift the flour, baking powder, and salt into a large mixing bowl.

4. Cut the shortening into the dry ingredients, using your fingertips to combine, until the dough resembles pea-size crumbs.

5. Add the hot milk to the dough, working in the liquid until a sticky ball forms.

6. Wrap the dough in plastic wrap and let it rest for 30 minutes at room temperature.

7. Divide equally into two large balls. Roll out each ball into an even disk ¾- to 1-inch thick. Put the dough on separate baking sheets.

8. Bake until completely cooked and golden brown, 20 to 25 minutes. After 10 minutes of baking, brush the bread with melted butter and put back in the oven for the remaining time, or until a toothpick inserted in the middle comes out clean.

9. Take out of oven, then brush again with melted butter. Serve warm with butter or with Vaquero Chili con Carne (page 134).

NOTE: To turn this into a sweet treat, add a healthy sprinkle of cinnamon and sugar after brushing with butter, and serve alongside hot chocolate or coffee.

FLOUR TORTILLAS

MAKES: 1 DOZEN (6- TO 8-INCH) OR 6 TO 8 (8-INCH) FLOUR TORTILLAS   PREP TIME: 45 MINUTES

COOK TIME: 3 TO 4 MINUTES PER TORTILLA

In my family, tortillas were an ever-present staple at breakfast, lunch, and dinner, and my mom made them fresh for *every* meal. But why was it flour when traditionally tortillas were made from corn? Turns out that the tortilla got caught up in the politics of the Catholic Church in the mid-1800s. This is a weighty subject. The Spanish Catholic Church needed wheat to make the host crackers for Mass, and there was no wheat. So they brought wheat to the New World in the 1500s. Later they realized the importance of corn to *los indios*—and used it as a power tool. "Eating like a native" was considered wrong by the Spaniards and they wanted to break the natives of their old ways to encourage them to embrace the new. In the process of trying to convert the native people to Christianity, the Church deemed corn unclean and not worthy for human consumption—to the extent that a law was created, stating that there could be no foods cooked with corn. Given that corn was a major staple, connecting the native people to the earth and their old way of life and beliefs, the public immediately revolted and refused to follow the law. But there were some lasting side effects, and one of those was the flour tortilla. It's astounding, as the corn tortilla originated in Mesoamerican times and was at the center of the gastronomical culture of Mexico, but even my Momo Davila (my grandmother) doesn't remember eating many corn tortillas.

3⅓ cups (1 pound) all-purpose flour, plus more for dusting

2 tablespoons baking powder

1 tablespoon salt

1 cup vegetable shortening

1½ cups hot water

1. Sift the flour, baking powder, and salt into a large mixing bowl.

2. Cut the shortening into the dry ingredients, using your fingertips to combine until its consistency resembles that of Play-Doh, by kneading and then folding repeatedly with your hands.

3. Add the hot water to the dough very slowly, similar to a small stream of water coming out of a faucet, working in the liquid with your hands until a sticky ball forms.

4. Wrap in plastic wrap and let rest for 30 minutes.

continued

5. Divide the dough into a dozen equal-size balls for medium-size tortillas, or six to eight balls for larger tortillas. Cover them again, this time with a damp cloth.

6. Use a countertop or wooden pastry board to roll out the dough. Lightly dust with flour to prevent sticking. Roll out each ball of dough into a disk about 1-inch thick. The shape will resemble a small hockey puck. To ensure a rounder disk, turn the tortilla a quarter-turn after each roll. You will be turning the tortilla three to four times to make it round, resulting in 6-inch disks for medium tortillas or 8-inch for large tortillas.

7. Heat a dry griddle or skillet over high heat for 5 minutes. Cook the tortillas one at a time until chalky looking with small charred spots where the tortilla has totally cooked through, about 30 seconds on each side. A properly cooked tortilla might rise and inflate like a balloon as all the ingredients react together. The balloon effect may not happen with every tortilla, but you will at least have a "bubbling" effect with most.

8. Place in a tortilla warmer or wrap in a lightly dampened towel as you cook the other tortillas.

9. Serve warm.

CORN TORTILLAS

MAKES **25 TO 30 (4- TO 5-INCH-DIAMETER) TORTILLAS**   PREP TIME: **2½ HOURS**

COOK TIME: **45 MINUTES PLUS 3 MINUTES PER TORTILLA**

In *tortilla de maíz nixtamal*, or corn tortillas, the corn is soaked and cooked in an alkaline solution, usually limewater or CAL (calcium hydroxide, a white powder found in Latin markets or online). I enjoy a corn tortilla on occasion but my emotional connection to the flavor is not deep, as I was raised on flour tortillas, and *molinas* (businesses that sold freshly ground masa) were not common, due to the popularity of flour. Despite this history, corn tortillas are one of the most important staples in Mexican cuisine, and are ever present.

3 cups white corn (dried yellow corn)

¼ cup CAL (white lime powder)

1. Clean the corn by cupping your hands and sifting it through your fingers to find and separate out any dirt.

2. Once cleaned, put the corn in a large stockpot with about 3 quarts of water. Stir in the CAL to cure the corn and make it easier to remove the husk or outer shell of the kernel. Bring the water to a boil. As the corn boils, the thin shell will separate from the corn. Maintain a rolling boil for 45 minutes.

3. Remove the stockpot from the heat and allow to cool, then chill the pot in your refrigerator for at least 2 hours, or until very cold. The corn must be cold, or it will spoil when you try to grind it.

4. Once the corn is cold, wash it with water, rubbing your hands over the submerged corn until it is very clean and the outer shells are removed.

5. Grind the corn in a molino (a hand-cranked corn and grain grinder), then grind it a second time. As you grind, add drops of water to ensure it stays moist directly where you are grinding it, but make sure not to add too much, as it will make it very sticky. After the first grind, the masa will look like small

continued

NOTE: If you're not up for making your own masa, you can buy dried corn flour and follow the directions on the bag to make a less flavorful but still fresh tortilla.

pebbles. Grind a second time to ensure that the masa is very fine. Make sure it is consistent and doesn't stick to your palms.

6. Roll the masa into golf ball–size balls.

7. Line the prensa (tortilla press) with plastic wrap to ensure the masa does not stick.

8. Individually press each masa ball in the prensa. Gently peel off the plastic wrap.

9. Cook each tortilla individually on a dry heavy skillet or comal over medium heat until it inflates or bubbles a bit and golden-brown spots appear, flipping twice, once every 30 seconds. Corn tortillas bubble up in a similar way to the flour tortilla, but they're not quite as puffy. Serve warm.

MOMO DAVILA'S GRIDDLE CORN CAKES

MAKES 10 TO 12 (3-INCH) CAKES   **PREP TIME: 10 TO 15 MINUTES**   **COOK TIME: 3 TO 5 MINUTES PER CAKE**

Some of life's best things are simple, and one of mine is the treasured memory of a corn cake in a paper towel, spread with butter. It was a comforting after-school snack. My *abuela*, Momo Davila, served this treat to all her grandchildren. It's the least complex recipe in this book, made with the greatest ingredient—love.

2 cups cornmeal

1 cup all-purpose flour

2 teaspoons salt

1½ teaspoons baking powder

1½ cups whole milk

1 cup vegetable shortening

Butter for serving

1. Sift the cornmeal, flour, salt, and baking powder into a large bowl.

2. Add the milk in a slow stream and mix until you get a pancake batter consistency.

3. Melt the shortening in a deep, cast-iron skillet over medium-high heat until it reaches 315° to 325°F.

4. With a large spoon, scoop the batter into the grease, no more than two or three spoonfuls at a time.

5. Cook the cake until golden brown and firm but not crisp, 1 minute per side, flipping it four times (twice on each side).

6. Remove the cake from the oil and place on a plate lined with paper towels. Repeat with the remaining batter.

7. Serve warm, topped with butter and a sprinkle of salt.

SOUTH TEXAS JALAPEÑO CHEESE CORN BREAD

MAKES **18 TO 24 SQUARES**   PREP TIME: **5 TO 10 MINUTES**   COOK TIME: **40 TO 45 MINUTES**

Corn is all around us in so many ways, as a staple in Texas and Mexico. You can find it all over our restaurant menus, from breads and sides to savory dishes and even desserts—so it can be incorporated into every course of a meal. This bread is a perfect example of corn's flexibility; adding cheese and jalapeños, we give it a Latin spin, and both sweet and spicy flavors. For a killer combination, serve this with Vaquero Chili con Carne (page 134).

½ cup vegetable oil, plus more for the Dutch oven

3⅓ cups (1 pound) all-purpose flour

3 cups (1 pound) cornmeal

¾ cup sugar

2 teaspoons baking powder

2 cups whole milk

2 large eggs

3 to 4 pickled jalapeño peppers, seeded and diced (optional)

1 cup grated mild Cheddar (optional)

1. Preheat the oven to 350°F and oil a large Dutch oven or casserole.

2. Sift the flour, cornmeal, sugar, and baking powder together into a large mixing bowl.

3. Stir in the milk, oil, and eggs, using a spoon or hand mixer, until just combined. Do not overmix or it will not rise.

4. Stir the diced jalapeños and grated cheese, if desired, into the batter.

5. Pour the batter into the prepared Dutch oven. Bake until the batter has risen and is solid, about 45 minutes. Check by inserting a toothpick in the center; if it comes out clean, the bread is fully baked. The bread may take up to an hour to bake, depending on your dish.

6. Remove from the oven and allow to cool for 10 to 15 minutes. Slice and serve.

SAUCES AND SALSAS

On the subject of barbecue in Texas, it's all about sauce on the side. And given our proximity to Mexico, every good Texan has a recipe for homemade salsa as well as barbecue sauce. At home, it was my mom's red picante table sauce that firmly held my attention. In this chapter, you'll find a sauce to suit your needs, whether sweet, spicy, tangy, or smoky.

DAVILA'S ORIGINAL BBQ SAUCE

MAKES 1 QUART; 12 TO 15 SERVINGS **PREP TIME: 10 MINUTES** **COOK TIME: 15 TO 20 MINUTES**

My grandmother proudly attests that this Texas-style, tomato-based BBQ sauce is the original recipe that my grandfather created. Davila's BBQ has been serving it since we opened our doors in 1959, and over the decades, we have produced countless gallons. While it has some similarities to other tomato-based sauces, the cumin and oregano bring in the Latin flavors that make the taste unique. We slather it on top of everything, as it pairs well with chicken, pork, beef, lamb, and even fish, such as salmon (see page 106).

1½ teaspoons margarine

½ cup tomato paste

½ cup ketchup

½ cup tomato juice

2 tablespoons Worcestershire sauce

¼ cup sugar

¼ cup cornstarch

2 tablespoons dill pickle juice

1 tablespoon prepared yellow mustard

¾ teaspoon freshly ground black pepper

¾ teaspoon garlic powder

¾ teaspoon ground cumin

½ teaspoon dried oregano

½ teaspoon salt

1. Melt the margarine in a large stockpot over medium low heat and stir in the tomato paste, ketchup, tomato juice, and Worcestershire sauce.

2. Combine the sugar, cornstarch, pickle juice, mustard, pepper, garlic powder, cumin, oregano, and salt in a large bowl. Mix well, until the sugar and salt are dissolved, then stir the mixture into the stockpot.

3. Cook over low heat until the sauce thickens, 10 minutes. Serve immediately or store in an airtight container in the refrigerator for up to 10 days.

NOTE: This recipe can be scaled up to make more for a big feast; we often make a full gallon.

DAVILA'S SPICY BBQ SAUCE

MAKES **1 QUART; 12 TO 15 SERVINGS**   PREP TIME: **10 MINUTES**   COOK TIME: **20 TO 25 MINUTES**

Savory with a bit of sweetness, this robust, spicy sauce is another Texas classic. Once again, in this kicked-up version of our original sauce, my grandfather tapped into his Latin roots with the use of cumin and oregano. It pairs well with poultry, beef, fish, or pork, served on the side, or for basting, but beware of adding it to an already spicy sausage as it will compound the heat!

1½ teaspoons margarine

½ cup tomato paste

½ cup ketchup

¼ cup tomato juice

2 tablespoons Worcestershire
   sauce

¼ cup cornstarch

¼ cup pickled jalapeño juice

2 tablespoons chopped chipotles

2 tablespoons tamarind or
   apricot marmalade

1 tablespoon prepared yellow
   mustard

¾ teaspoon cayenne pepper

1 teaspoon freshly ground black
   pepper

1 teaspoon garlic powder

1 teaspoon ground cumin

½ teaspoon dried oregano

1½ teaspoons sugar

½ teaspoon salt

1. Melt the margarine in a large stockpot over medium-low heat, then stir in the tomato paste, ketchup, tomato juice, and Worcestershire sauce.

2. Combine the cornstarch, pickled jalapeño juice, chipotle, marmalade, mustard, cayenne, black pepper, garlic powder, cumin, oregano, sugar, and salt in a large bowl. Mix well, until the sugar and salt are dissolved, then stir the mixture into the stockpot.

3. Cook over low heat until the sauce thickens, 10 minutes. Serve immediately or store in an airtight container in the refrigerator for up to 10 days.

NOTE: This recipe can be scaled up to make more for a big feast; we often make a full gallon.

FIRE-ROASTED TOMATO, ONION, AND SERRANO SALSA

MAKES **4 CUPS**   PREP TIME: **45 MINUTES (TO HEAT THE FIRE TO RED EMBERS)**   COOK TIME: **6 MINUTES**

This recipe exudes simplicity, because it's all about the method, which is practically primal, but requires a certain amount of finesse. Cooking directly on the coals imparts a different layer of flavor than straight grilling. You'll find it brings the sugars forward while caramelizing the onions and tomatoes, yet it also intensifies the spiciness of the serranos. "*Se amargan si se queman*," as my abuelo would always say—"they're bitter if they burn," so watch carefully as you cook to blacken and caramelize the vegetables but not fully char or burn them. I like to serve this dish with fajitas so that I can cook all the ingredients on the same fire, but it's great simply served with chips or as a topping for a favorite dish.

3 large serrano peppers

½ pound ripe tomatoes

2 large, sweet yellow onions

1 garlic head

¼ cup chopped fresh cilantro

2 teaspoons salt

1. Prepare the fire: A coal fire is ready when burning with red coals; wood fires are ready when burning with red and white coals. (If it's white to ashes, you've burned too long.) Alternatively, you can use a broiler to approximate this recipe, turning the vegetables frequently until all sides are charred.

2. Place each vegetable individually, whole, uncut, and unpeeled, on the red coals. Turn the vegetables as needed when the skin blackens and caramelizes. Remove from the fire when all sides are blackened but before they are crisped or fully charred and burned, 3 to 6 minutes total, depending on the vegetable. Watch closely: the smaller the vegetable, the less time it will take to cook. Remove the vegetables from the coals and set aside to cool. Do not refrigerate.

3. Remove the charred skin, using a terry cloth: Place each vegetable in the middle of the cloth and gently rub the skin off. It is important that you do not rinse the vegetables, as rinsing will eliminate flavor. An alternative method is to cover the vegetables with plastic wrap and allow them to cool in

continued

NOTE: If you can get your hands on one, the use of the molcajete lends a unique, slightly chunky texture that a blender or any other mechanized kitchen tool just can't deliver.

the steam, and then peel by hand. Remove the stems from the peppers, and from the tomatoes if needed. If you'd like a less spicy sauce, you can also remove some or all of the seeds from the peppers at this point.

4. Put the vegetables in a molcajete (or blender, if you must) and mash until the vegetables are the desired salsa consistency (chunky or smooth).

5. Season with cilantro and salt and serve.

MINI ASADO STYLE FOR VEGGIES

When making an asado-style fire (see page 27) for cooking vegetables, what I do here at the restaurant is pick up a shovel, get the amount of coals that I need out of the fire, and cook them right on the shovel—in lieu of having to build a whole second fire in a separate grill. So, a note to the reader: If you're already grilling, try out my hack; just keep small children and animals away!

TOMATILLO SALSA (GREEN SAUCE)

MAKES **4 CUPS**   PREP TIME: **45 MINUTES (TO HEAT THE FIRE TO RED EMBERS)**   COOK TIME: **6 MINUTES**

This salsa follows essentially the same technique as the Fire-Roasted Tomato, Onion, and Serrano Salsa (page 174); however, this one is all about the tangy taste. The citrus flavor profile means it pairs extremely well with pork, chicken, or even fish. The risk/reward (and what makes it fun) is playing with fire, using the hot ember cooking technique! This sauce can also be used for enchiladas or over eggs and strips of crunchy tortillas to make *chilaquiles*.

2 pounds tomatillos (ripe, with husks)

3 large serrano peppers

1 whole garlic head

½ cup chopped fresh cilantro

2 teaspoons salt

1. Prepare the fire: A coal fire is ready when burning with red coals; wood fires are ready when burning with red and white coals. (If it's white to ashes, you've burned too long.) Alternatively, you can use a broiler to approximate this recipe, turning the vegetables frequently until all sides are charred.

2. Place each vegetable individually, whole, uncut, and unpeeled, on the red coals. Turn the vegetables as needed when the vegetable skin blackens and caramelizes. Remove from the fire when all sides are blackened but before they are crisped or fully charred and burned, 3 to 6 minutes total, depending on the vegetable. Watch closely; the smaller the vegetable, the less time it will take to cook on the fire. Remove the vegetables from the coals and set aside to allow to cool. Do not refrigerate.

3. Remove the charred skin, using a terry cloth: Place each vegetable in the middle of the cloth and gently rub the skin off. It is important that you do not rinse the vegetables, as rinsing will eliminate flavor. An alternative method is to cover the vegetables with plastic wrap and allow them to cool in the steam, and then peel by hand. Remove the stems from the peppers, and from the tomatillos if needed. If you'd like a less spicy sauce, you can also remove some or all of the seeds from

continued

the peppers at this point.

4. Put the vegetables in a molcajete (or blender) and mash until the vegetables are a smooth salsa consistency.

5. Season the salsa with cilantro and salt and serve.

MAMA DAVILA'S SALSA PICANTE (RED TABLE SAUCE)

MAKES **2 CUPS, SERVES 6 TO 8**   PREP TIME: **15 TO 20 MINUTES**

Albeit very simple, with few ingredients, this recipe comes from my mom and holds a special place in my heart. I grew up eating salsa picante with almost every meal. It was ever present as a table condiment, and topped everything, including eggs in breakfast tacos. It added a tomato-filled spicy kick to our *picadillo* (ground beef), or was served as straight-up salsa with chips. It will always be my favorite salsa, and I'm not alone—this is the table sauce that's commonly served at any and every meal throughout Texas, whether you are of Hispanic origin or not. Serve it with fresh tortilla chips, over tacos or eggs, or with other savory dishes and meats.

2 whole fresh tomatoes, roughly chopped

3 serrano peppers, stemmed, seeded, and chopped

1 medium white onion, roughly chopped

1 (16-ounce) can whole tomatoes

1½ teaspoons minced fresh cilantro, or to taste

Pinch of granulated garlic

Salt and freshly ground black pepper

1. Combine the fresh tomatoes, serrano peppers, onion, and canned tomatoes in a food processor or blender. Pulse quickly to blend all the ingredients, making sure not to whip or add air.

2. Stir in the cilantro and granulated garlic, then season with salt and pepper to taste. Serve immediately or store in an airtight container in the refrigerator for up to 4 days.

GUAJILLO SALSA

MAKES **2 CUPS**   COOK TIME: **15 MINUTES**

This salsa is unique because it has just the right balance of heat and tanginess. The dark guajillos and the robust tomatillos both cook on the embers and come together to form the least spicy of the salsas in this book. But, make no mistake, this is the most versatile one, too. I like it on any meat. It's a popular offering at our local taco spots and I eat it on my eggs because it has just enough spunk to wake me up without burning my tongue.

6 guajillo chiles, stems removed

1 pound tomatillos, husks and
   stems removed

2 garlic cloves, peeled

1 teaspoon minced fresh cilantro

1 teaspoon salt

1. Prepare coals asado style (see page 27)—red coals, not ashy white ones.

2. Using a long set of tongs, put the chiles on the coals. Turn them every few seconds until they inflate but are not charred, about 15 seconds total.

3. On the same coals, cook the tomatillos until blistering but not yet rendering their juices, 2 to 3 minutes. Remove from the coals and allow them to cool in the refrigerator for 5 minutes.

4. Place the chiles and garlic in a molcajete (or blender) and mash into a paste.

5. Remove the tomatillos from the refrigerator and add them to the molcajete. Mash into a chunky consistency.

6. Add the chopped cilantro and salt and mash to incorporate.

PICO DE GALLO

MAKES **2 CUPS**   PREP TIME: **10 MINUTES**

There are countless interpretations and variations of this condiment. From habaneros to mangoes, the ingredients can be from one's region or given a twist with different types of fruit. This version is great with fajitas or for any grilled item because it is sweet, sour, and spicy.

3 medium tomatoes, cut into ½-inch dice

½ white onion, cut into ½-inch dice

2 serrano peppers, seeded and diced

2 sprigs cilantro, chopped

Juice of 1 lime

1 teaspoon salt

Combine all the ingredients in a medium bowl just before serving, as this recipe is best when freshly prepared. Not intended for use the next day.

ACKNOWLEDGMENTS

Sarah (my wife-to-be): My self-proclaimed biggest fan and supporter, thank you. Without your unwavering love and personal sacrifices to allow me to chase my dreams, I couldn't have done this. This book is something we created together, as we begin to share our lives together. I can't wait for what else life has in store for us. This is just the beginning, my love.

My mom, Haydee, and dad, Edward: Thank you for making me believe that I could do anything, and for your continuous, countless hours at the restaurant, holding it all down when I had to leave and tend to meetings or filming in California or New York. And thank you for life guidance and leading by example.

My grandmother, Geronima Davila, and late grandfather, Raul Davila: You are my inspirations for this book, and I dedicate it to y'all. This book immortalizes your legacy and passion for food and family. Thank you for everything you have given me.

My late grandmother, Gracie DeLaGarza, and grandfather, David DeLaGarza: Both of you always had such a loving and kind spirit. I draw my artistic side and my love of music from you.

My sister, Delissa, and my brother-in-law, Joey: Thank you for always being there for me, and, most of all, for giving me beautiful nieces and a nephew: Julissa, Juliana, and Jacob.

My brother, Edward, and sister-in-law, Carmen: Thank you for pushing me and never letting me fail, and for giving me beautiful nieces and a nephew: Grace, Audrey, and Edward.

My nieces and nephews: Just remember that beyond the sky is the limit. I can't wait to see all that you accomplish.

My extended family: Thank you to my entire family of cousins, aunts, and uncles. I wouldn't be who I am without your guidance along the way.

My father-in-law, Tom Dozier: For treating me like a son and opening up the beloved ranch to my crazy cooking and outdoor sessions.

My mother-in-law, Drew Dozier: For your inspiration, and for supporting me 100 percent as a fellow book author.

Countless present and former employees: Pati, Antonio, Maria, Ana, Alicia, Daniel, Odelmis, Llayenis: Without you sharing your knowledge, stories, and expertise, this book would not have been possible. Your hard work and dedication are beyond words . . .

Alex Perez and his late brother Ariel Perez: Alex, I look up to you for strength. Knowing what you've been through and where you came from gives me inspiration. Ariel, rest in peace.

Jason and Laura Nichols, Steven Paprocki, Tobias Soto, and Mr. and Mrs. Tirado: Thank you for sharing your time and effort to help make this book come together. Your helping hands are endlessly valuable.

Goldie McKinney: To my "third grandma," thank you.

Dan Napier: For showing me that someone from our little city of Seguin can go "big-time."

The Seguin community and all of our loyal customers: Thank you for supporting my family and me and for being so good to us. "It takes a village to raise a child."

Melissa Guerra: You're an inspiration and a Latin history guru, thank you for your advice as a fellow author (and for your beautiful food props, too!).

Julia Rothensfelds: Thank you for your incredible knowledge of this cultural food history and your invaluable friendship.

Jonathan Woytek: For showing me that my limits were only what I set upon myself.

The Countryman Press: Ann Treistman and Aurora Bell, from the bottom of my heart, thanks to you and your excellent team, including Devorah Backman, Maya Baran, Devon Zahn, and LeAnna Weller Smith, for your unwavering and singular belief in this book and for the outstanding editorial, design, PR, and sales contributions.

Pauline Stevens: For your special eye for the perfect shot.

Karla Toye: For your superb food styling.

Greg Quail: Gratitude for discovering me and placing me in front of all the top people, to land me where I am today.

Sharon Bowers: Thank you for knowing the right timing for my success and for pairing me with Ann Volkwein, who was the perfect co-author.

Melissa Campbell: For your persistence in pushing me as a talent.

Ann Volkwein: Thank you for going above and beyond "writing" this book. Thank you for making this book a project of passion. Thank you for your invaluable insight on the food, literary, and entertainment world.

Snoop, Oso, Rose, Goose: The 4 little furry dog children who greet me every day with a smile no matter what!

And . . .
To everyone not mentioned personally, please know that every time I see you at the restaurant, at the grocery store, or anywhere else, I am reminded of how thankful I am that so many people have helped me along in life and have joined me on my path.

Thank you Lord for giving me a beautiful world. From the fruits of the land to the animals we raise, everything has worked together seamlessly since the beginning of time, and writing this book allowed me to see that and appreciate everything we harvest.

INDEX

Note: Page references in *italics* indicate photographs.